Blue Collar Resumes

By

Steven A. Provenzano,
CPRW

Career Press
Franklin Lakes, NJ

Copyright © 1999 by Steve Provenzano

All rights reserved under the Pan-American and International Copyright Conventions. This book may not be reproduced, in whole or in part, in any form or by any means electronic or mechanical, including photocopying, recording, or by any information storage and retrieval system now known or hereafter invented, without written permission from the publisher, The Career Press.

BLUE COLLAR RESUMES
Cover design by Hub Graphics
Typesetting by Eileen Munson
Printed in the U.S.A. by Book-mart Press

To order this title, please call toll-free 1-800-CAREER-1 (NJ and Canada: 201-848-0310) to order using VISA or MasterCard, or for further information on books from Career Press.

The Career Press, Inc., 3 Tice Road, PO Box 687, Franklin Lakes, NJ 07417

Library of Congress Cataloging-in-Publication Data

Provenzano, Steven.
    Blue collar resumes / by Steve Provenzano.
        p.   cm.
    Includes index.
    ISBN 1-56414-412-7 (pbk.)
    1. Résumés (Employment)   2. Job hunting.   3. Blue collar workers.
I. Title.
HF5383.P733   1999
808'.06665—dc21

99-22502

Dedicated to
my family and friends,
the finest in the world.

Special thanks to Steve Burdan, vice president, writer,
and tireless worker, *A ADVANCED* Resume Service, Inc.

Contents

A Better Job

Begins

On Paper

Congratulations for picking up this book! The new millennium is upon us, and there's no better time to create a better future for yourself.

I'm writing this book for the so-called "blue collar" workers, the people who do some of the hardest, most essential, and least recognized work in the world.

Just about every major company, from Motorola to General Motors to Pillsbury, relies on millions of blue collar workers to assemble, repair, stock, and deliver what they sell. Without this essential work force, America would grind to a halt, a fact that many believe is lost to some of the people who run those big companies.

But as the 21st century begins, there are signs of change. At the time of this writing, unemployment is down to less than 5 percent, and some companies are feeling the pinch of a tight labor market. At my resume service, I get calls every week from employment agencies looking to fill positions for drivers, factory workers, and a multitude of other skilled trades. Industry analysts such as Tom Peters have spoken for years about the essential role of blue collar and service workers, because in many cases, they have the most direct contact with the most important person in business: the customer.

Finally, after all the cutbacks and layoffs of the early 1990s, blue collar workers are in greater demand than ever before. They are demanding—and getting—higher pay and better benefits.

But there's a catch. Employers are now looking for people with wider skill sets to work longer hours, and they expect higher quality work and devotion to their company. In other words, they want more bang for their buck.

Many expect a focused, hard-working team of eight to do what used to be done by 10 just a year before. They also want people with good communication skills. And often the first impression you will give an employer of your communication skills is on your resume—so it better be good!

A new philosophy

Because my staff and I write resumes just about every day, I meet a wide range of people looking for better jobs. After writing more than 4,000 resumes, I'm still amazed at the variety of work that people do. But everybody who comes to me has one thing in common—they all want a better job. They can't, however, get a new job without an interview—and they can't get an interview without a great resume.

People still walk into my office and give me hand-written notes on dirty scratch paper. They scribble out a basic history—where and when they worked and a short outline of their daily duties. I tell them that's a start, and then I ask "The Question":

What do you really want to DO in your next job?

Some people are surprised when I ask this, and you'd be surprised at the answers I get. Many assume they will keep doing the same exact work they were doing for their previous or current employer, until they start to really think about this question.

But no two jobs, even if they have the same job title, are exactly the same. That's why it's essential to look at the *types* of skills you would like to use on the next job, and then create a resume that will get you in that *type* of position.

A new approach

Most people think a resume is just an outline of old jobs and educational background (that's what I call a "job list," or history of your working life). To some extent that's true, because your work history is an essential part of your resume (more on this later). But there's a new approach to resume writing that can help open doors to the really *good* jobs, assist you in increasing your income, and help you enjoy what you're doing 40 to 50 hours every week. To accomplish this, your resume must consistently:

·Highlight and Sell
your Skills and Abilities

This may sound like a simple concept, but think about it: Does the average "job list" resume really highlight your skills, your talents, and what you can really can bring to your next job? Usually not, and for one important reason—when you send out a "job list" resume, you're telling people what you've done for your previous employers, but you're not really telling *what you can do for your next employer.*

And that's really what this book is all about—helping you identify and *sell* your most important and relevant skills, abilities, knowledge, and training on paper. With so many people looking for new jobs (yes, even with low unemployment, competition for the *best* jobs is still tough) it's essential to create a high-impact resume that develops and sells your skills and abilities.

Simple and basic? Or ineffective?

I can't tell you just how many people call my office and say they want a "simple" or "basic" resume. For some reason, they think there's something magical about those words. Most people come to me with brief descriptions of their work history and education. Initially, they want it typeset so they can run 100 copies at the local office supply store.

Whenever I hear the words "simple" or "basic," I stop them in their tracks when I tell them, "We'll make it *effective*." Never underestimate the power of a few "basic" words.

What you're up against

Did you know that the average one-inch job advertisement in the Sunday paper can draw hundreds of resumes? Research tells us that most of these resumes have only a few seconds to grab the reader's attention.

Job Search Facts

A survey of 150 executives from the nation's 1,000 largest companies was conducted by Accountemps/Robert Half. Can you believe that 70 percent said they spend two minutes *or less* reviewing an applicant's resume? That's why your resume must become an attention-getting *advertisement,* and not just another job history.

The resume screening process

Let's face it. Resumes are often used as a tool for "weeding out" potential candidates. No matter how many job openings a company may have, there simply isn't the time or staff to interview every single person who would like to be interviewed. And so the people in human resources, or your potential boss, will sift through resumes received from internal job postings, employment agencies, and—yes—want ads.

When I worked in human resources as a corporate recruiter, I did what many of my peers did—I sifted through the day's resumes and made three separate piles. I labeled them "Great," "Possible," and "Never," and first called in people from the "Great" stack for interviews. Often, I ended up throwing out not just the "Never" pile, but the "Possible" pile, as well.

After thousands of face-to-face interviews of potential candidates, I've learned one of the most important facts of job-hunting: The best person doesn't always get hired. Rather, it's the person who presents himself or herself with clarity, precision, and impact in the resume and, later, in the interview.

Most resumes are quickly scanned (visually by a resume screener, typically in the human resources department, or electronically via a computer) for essential words that relate to the job requirements, including, for example, certifications or proficiencies with types of computer software. HR screeners may also look for an overall knowledge of the specific industry. Assuming this is found, they may then check for such items as a steady work history (not too many jobs in too short a time) or educational background and training.

If the initial glance passes muster, the HR representative may pass along your resume, with several others, to the hiring manager. Typically, that manager is the direct supervisor over the open position, and will make the final decision about whom to call in for interviews. The initial interviews are then conducted by the HR department, and a short list of candidates is created.

Finally, about three to five candidates will be interviewed by the hiring manager (sometimes with other department managers present) and a decision is made to offer the position to the candidate who best suits their needs and their payroll budget. As you can see, there are plenty of opportunities throughout the process to eliminate resumes and candidates that don't stand out as strong contenders!

The need for accuracy

As noted earlier, research shows that the average resume has only a few seconds to catch the reader's interest. For the same reason, brevity, accuracy, and overall appearance are key to a successful resume. If you're not sure how to spell a word, look it up. If you don't know how to type accurately, hire a professional typist.

Job Search Facts

Proofread, Proofread, Proofread!!! OfficeTeam conducted a survey of 150 human resources and other managers from the nation's 1,000 largest companies. Results revealed that 76 percent said they would not hire candidates who have one or two typographical errors on their resume, and 45 percent said it would take only one typo to eliminate a candidate from consideration. Be careful what you send—have family and friends proofread your resume from top to bottom, and bottom to top.

Accuracy and quality of writing is essential. Nothing turns off an employer more than basic spelling or grammar mistakes on a resume. The subconscious impression is, "If this person can't even produce a decent resume, how could he or she possibly perform this job well?" Later on in this book, we'll offer some proofreading suggestions, as well as some hints for designing and creating an attractive and readable resume.

Whether you have years of experience or are straight out of school, you can choose to present yourself through your resume in an average way—or in an outstanding way. The difference between a good resume and a *great* resume may just be the "foot in the door" you need to land those job interviews—which will lead to more opportunities for *better* job offers.

Taking stock of yourself

I truly believe that writing an effective resume is a process of self-discovery, so I try to create personal advertisements for the people who walk into my office. I assume they have certain abilities, skills, and training that will be useful in their next job. It's my job to identify the best talents that person has to offer, and then *develop* those talents on paper—otherwise they're not much use in the job-hunt process.

Because I'm not sitting across from you, it's your job to take a step back and take an honest look at what you can really bring your next employer.

You must take stock of your knowledge and accomplishments in your chosen field and decide what to develop, what to downplay, and what to leave out altogether. Relax, it's easier than you might think, and the worksheets in Chapter 1 should help.

This discovery process will prove even more valuable down the road, when you start to go on job interviews. It can help get you ready for interview questions and can actually create new career choices, when you see that your skills may be applicable to entirely new industries.

Your resume is one of the few aspects in your job search over which you have complete control, and it is one of your most valuable assets. During my career seminars, I tell people that their resume can be the most important document they will ever have: more important than their driver's license, their passport, or even their birth certificate, because no other document can have such an impact on income and, most importantly, where and how they spend 40 to 50 hours of their life every week.

Of course, mailing or e-mailing your resume isn't the only way to get an interview. There's personal networking with friends, former co-workers, and clients, and cold-calling target companies. Still, a resume is almost always essential, no matter which method you use to land job interviews.

Job Search Facts

Market studies show that 60 to 80 percent of professionals get their jobs through informal referrals. About 15 percent are filled through search firms, 10 percent through mass mailings and only about 5 percent through published advertisements! Like the saying goes, sometimes it's who you know that matters, but you will always need a great resume to pass on through a personal contact.

Some new perspectives

Remember, your resume will not get you a job—only *you* can do that—but it certainly can prevent you from getting one. If your resume does *not* effectively sell your skills and showcase your experience and achievements, you can bet that there are plenty of others in the stack of resumes on the hiring manager's desk that do! An excellent presentation of your talents can increase your chances of getting an interview, where you get the chance to personally sell your qualifications.

A "great" resume is defined differently for everyone, given their particular situation and the job market. That's why there are very few hard and fast rules about the "perfect" resume. What's perfect is what will work best for you in *your* situation. Just because a resume "style" or "format" seems to work for someone you know doesn't mean it'll work for you!

Interview yourself!

You must now become your own professional writer. Because I can't sit across from you and ask questions about your experience and education, you must do it yourself. This requires honesty and objectivity. Are you really proficient at *everything* you do? Of course not. On the other hand, don't take any of your applicable experience for granted. It can be a mistake to assume an employer knows what you can do simply because they are already in that particular business.

Help from a professional service?

A Certified Professional Resume Writer can probably improve your resume. CPRWs must pass a challenging test and meet rigid criteria before receiving certification from the Professional Association of Resume Writers (PARW).

I've created resumes for some great technical writers who were amazed at the results. That's because I make resumes my specialty. If I needed written documents on integrated circuit design or computer programs, I'd hire a technical writer. If I needed someone to run a company, I'd hire the best executive I could find.

A good CPRW may be able to write better about you simply because he or she is *not* you. The best ones know what employers want to see, and may even have experience in human resources departments of major businesses. The writer can take an objective look at your background, ask you numerous, in-depth questions, and create a marketing piece that has a better chance of impressing an employer and increasing your chances of getting a personal interview.

When considering a professional resume writer, ask about CPRW certification, years of experience, and whether the individual can give you good references. Make sure the person works out of a regular, full-time office, and that this isn't just a sideline business. Additional experience in human resources, recruiting, or top management is a plus.

If the resume writer offers you a flat fee over the phone, remember that this can easily change when you walk in the door. The writer should offer a free resume analysis and not even try to quote prices without seeing what kind of work is involved for your resume.

Making the most of this book

Blue Collar Resumes is designed to help you gather and organize your skills and abilities, and market them to employers with the goal of landing interviews. Using sample resumes and the latest ideas about effective resume writing, you will be able to sift through your entire work history, then extract and develop key points about your talents and sell them to the reader—your prospective employer!

Chapters 1 through 8 will walk you through the process, from helping you evaluate your past work experience, education, and skill development and translating them into powerful selling points, to choosing the most effective format and organization of your achievements, to designing and printing the finished product, to making job contacts.

Additionally, this book includes 126 resume examples, based on resumes that helped my clients land jobs! Of course, the names and particulars have been changed, but the circumstances of each resume represented in this book are "real-life." Read through the resumes, study the different formats, designs, and organizations. You can pick and choose elements you like and create your own job-winning resume.

In addition, the resume examples in the book reflect a spectrum of careers and job descriptions. You may note that some of the jobs represented are not traditional "blue collar" jobs.

The definition of "blue collar" has certainly changed over the years. The term used to be interchangeable with "manual laborer." But with advances in technology, traditional blue collar workers—factory workers, assemblers, and construction laborers—are often required to perform technological tasks that have little to do with manual labor.

For instance, an automobile assembly line worker may now need to program and operate complex, robotic, and CNC equipment for a specific assembly line operation. In the past, products were assembled with basic tools—hammers, socket wrenches, handheld welders, and soldering equipment. Today, high-tech assembly lines require trained personnel to program and operate advanced equipment for high-speed production and quality control. Of course, these workers still get their hands dirty every day, But for the most part, many jobs that were once labeled "blue collar" require less brawn and more brain.

I realize that many of you reading this book may aspire to jobs in other fields that are not traditionally considered "blue collar." Perhaps you're looking to use newly acquired skills in staff management, quality control, or computer systems. That's why I've included a wide range of job examples—including secretaries, customer service representatives and clerical positions, data entry clerks—that indeed blur the traditional lines of white-collar, blue-collar until the collar becomes somewhat "gray."

People in these "gray-collar" positions tend to have more direct contact with both customers and white collar workers within the company, such as executives and sales representatives. These workers, who are often categorized as "clerical," "support staff," or "customer service" workers, are becoming more recognized as essential to the company's bottom line success. They often deal with the most important person in the corporate food chain—the customer.

In addition, I've included resume samples that reflect other careers outside the traditional blue collar spectrum. You'll find resume samples for dancers, caterers, travel agents, and medical workers as well.

No matter what income level you're at, or what type of work you do, this guide is designed to help you increase your income through career advancement and improvement. Go ahead and make notes in the margins, fill out the worksheets (or make copies of them so you can change, update, and improve as necessary), or circle phrases and ideas that apply specifically to your situation— as long as this isn't a library book! The point is this—*use it!* The more you involve yourself in the process, the better you'll understand what makes a successful resume—and the better your final resume will be!

Get Started: Assessing Your Skills

Whenever I write a resume, I think about what runs through the minds of prospective employers as they read the resume:

Why should I interview this candidate?

Employers must see reasons to consider you as soon as they pick up your resume. Keep throwing reasons at them! The more reasons you give them, the better. Put yourself in their shoes, and pretend you're reading your own resume: Is it enough to write that you are skilled in customer service? Or do you need to be specific? ("Personally communicate with staff, management, and customers regarding company procedures and product lines.")

Take some time to think about how you would answer every employer's question: "Why should I call you in?"

In the following pages, you'll find worksheets that will help you identify your skills, work achievements, and experience—in detail. This may be the most important step in developing your resume. Not only will it help you pull out the accomplishments that will answer the questions of prospective employers, it will help *you* learn more about yourself and make you more confident as you pursue exciting new opportunities and walk into job interviews.

Take some time as you work through these pages. If necessary, review performance evaluations from previous jobs, ask co-workers for honest assessments of your skills and strengths—and give some thought to which aspects of your work you're best at and, most importantly, love the most.

YOUR PERSONAL INVENTORY

Name

First _____ Middle _____

Last _____

Address

Street _____

City _____ State _____ Zip _____

Telephone: Area Code _____ / _____

E-mail Address: _____

Desired Position or Industry: _____

_____

_____

_____

_____

_____

_____

_____

_____

EMPLOYMENT (List most relevant jobs first)

From   Company _____

____ 19____ City & State _____

To   Type of Business _____

____ 19____ Product or Service _____

Positions or Titles _____

Responsibilities & Duties _____

_____

_____

Supervisory Duties _____

_____

Accomplishments or Major Achievements _____

_____

From   Company _____

____ 19____ City & State _____

To   Type of Business _____

____ 19____ Product or Service _____

Positions or Titles _____

Responsibilities & Duties _____

_____

_____

Supervisory Duties _____

_____

Accomplishments or Major Achievements _____

_____

EMPLOYMENT

From   Company _____

____ 19 ____ City & State _____

To   Type of Business _____

___ 19 ___ Product or Service _____

Positions or Titles _____

Responsibilities & Duties _____

_____

_____

Supervisory Duties _____

_____

Accomplishments or Major Achievements _____

_____

From   Company _____

____ 19 ____ City & State _____

To   Type of Business _____

____ 19 ____ Product or Service _____

Positions or Titles _____

Responsibilities & Duties _____

_____

_____

Supervisory Duties _____

_____

Accomplishments or Major Achievements _____

_____

EMPLOYMENT

From   Company _____

____ 19 ____ City & State _____

To   Type of Business _____

____ 19 ____ Product or Service _____

Positions or Titles _____

Responsibilities & Duties _____

_____

_____

Supervisory Duties _____

_____

Accomplishments or Major Achievements _____

_____

From   Company _____

____ 19____ City & State _____

To   Type of Business _____

____ 19____ Product or Service _____

Positions or Titles _____

Responsibilities & Duties _____

_____

_____

Supervisory Duties _____

_____

Accomplishments or Major Achievements _____

_____

EDUCATION (Most recent first)

College _____

City/State _____

Degree _____ Year _____

Major _____ Minor _____ GPA _____

Course work/Studies _____

_____

Achievements/Activities _____

_____

College _____

City/State _____

Degree _____ Year _____

Major _____ Minor _____ GPA _____

Course work/Studies _____

_____

Achievements/Activities _____

_____

Awards/Scholarships _____

_____

Seminars and Special Training _____

_____

_____

_____

_____

_____

_____

Vocational/Trade School _____

City/State _____

Certificate _____ Dates Attended _____

Awards/Achievements _____

_____

Special Jobs/Equipment _____

_____

Vocational/Trade School _____

City/State _____

Certificate _____ Dates Attended _____

Awards/Achievements _____

_____

Special Jobs/Equipment _____

_____

High School _____

Dates Attended _____

City/State _____

Achievements/Activities _____

_____

Military Service _____

Dates Enlisted _____

Special Skills/Training _____

_____

_____

Awards/Achievements _____

_____

Honorable Discharge? _____ Rank _____

PROFESSIONAL MEMBERSHIPS

Organization _____ Dates _____

Offices Held _____

Duties/Responsibilities _____

_____

Skills Acquired _____

_____

Organization _____ Dates _____

Offices Held _____

Duties/Responsibilities _____

_____

Skills Acquired _____

_____

Organization _____ Dates _____

Offices Held _____

Duties/Responsibilities _____

_____

Skills Acquired _____

_____

Organization _____ Dates _____

Offices Held _____

Duties/Responsibilities _____

_____

Skills Acquired _____

_____

COMMUNITY SERVICES & VOLUNTEER ACTIVITIES

Organization _____

Offices/Titles Held _____

City/State _____ Dates _____

Specific activities in which you were involved and skills utilized

_____

_____

Organization _____

Offices/Titles Held _____

City/State _____ Dates _____

Specific activities in which you were involved and skills utilized

_____

_____

Organization _____

Offices/Titles Held _____

City/State _____ Dates _____

Specific activities in which you were involved and skills utilized

_____

_____

PERSONAL INTERESTS, SPORTS & HOBBIES

_____

_____

_____

_____

References
Business

Name _____ Title _____

Company Name _____

Company Address _____

_____

Telephone, Office _____ Home (optional) _____

Name _____ Title _____

Company Name _____

Company Address _____

_____

Telephone, Office _____ Home (optional) _____

Name _____ Title _____

Company Name _____

Company Address _____

_____

Telephone, Office _____ Home (optional) _____

Personal:

Name _____ Profession _____

Telephone, Office _____ Home (optional) _____

Name _____ Profession _____

Telephone, Office _____ Home (optional) _____

Name _____ Profession _____

Telephone, Office _____ Home (optional) _____

Organize Your Resume to Make You Shine

If there's one idea I hope to convince you of in this book, it's that your resume is your opportunity to promote yourself, to put yourself in the very best light to communicate your unique achievements, special skills, and one-of-a-kind experiences. It's your chance to sell yourself!

And because each of us has different experiences, skills, and achievements, there isn't *one, perfect way* to organized a resume. In this chapter, we'll take a look at the three most common resume formats to determine which may work best for *you.*

1. Chronological format. The *chronological* format is the most commonly used resume format. It emphasizes your work history, positioning it either first on the resume or following the Job Objective section or Title. The employment history is listed in the order of the most recent job first.

Most people use this format because it is simple and straightforward—and it is what most human resources professionals are used to seeing. If you've had a steady work history and you've gained skills and achievements as you have progressed, this might be a good format for you.

The main problem with this format, however, is that it emphasizes most *recent* experience. So, if you're applying for a position as a manicurist, for example, and your most recent job was in retail sales, your resume might get tossed in the reject pile before the reader notices that you'd been doing nails for 15 years prior to your last job.

The chronological format may also be troublesome for the person who has had an erratic job history—gaps in employment are made apparent by the chronological listing of jobs, and may raise questions in the reader's mind.

2. Functional format. A functional format begins with a listing or summary of your skills, rather than an Employment section, with the purpose of communicating abilities and strengths that the prospective employer might be seeking. The only detail about job history will be as it relates to the skills you highlight—and it may not include work dates or names of employers.

For example, if you were seeking a job as a cook for a catering company, you might list that you'd cooked meals for 400 people for a six-month period while at sea. You wouldn't, however, mention that this was part of your tour of duty in the Navy 12 years ago.

Often, job-seekers use this format to downplay gaps in work history or the fact that they're jumping into a new career. Homemakers or military personnel returning to the work force often use this format. Because a functional resume can send up red flags to readers—who may suspect that you're trying to hide something—you may want to consider carefully before using it.

3. Combination format. Here's the one I like the most, because it's a combination of what's best of the functional and chronological formats. Typically, a combination resume begins with a strong Experience or Profile section to sell your skills and emphasize achievements that pertain to the job you're seeking. Then you can demonstrate how you applied or acquired these skills by following it with a Job History or Employment section.

This is the format that typically works best for my clients. It showcases the applicable skills and accomplishments, and reassures the reader that the candidate has nothing to hide by offering details about work history. Often in the combination format, job-seekers will also incorporate volunteer jobs and nonpaid experience into their chronology of jobs and experience. This is fine, as long as you don't try to lead the reader into thinking they were paid positions.

We've found the combination format to be a winning format for most people—many clients say that they've received a 20-percent to 40-percent response rate. In other words, many will get two to four interviews for every 10 resumes they send out!

Reaching for the ideal position

Imagine yourself in the ideal position: What would you actually be *doing* day to day and hour to hour? When I was an HR director and reviewing resumes, my requirements were simple—the candidate had to:

- Demonstrate on paper that he or she had considered the requirements of the position.
- Effectively pre-sort experience and information in terms of relevance.
- Identify his or her most relevant skills and abilities.
- Give a good, clear, concise overview of transferable skills and abilities.

Because time is tight during a job search, and the competition can be intense, the trick is to get as much *relevant* information across to the reader as quickly as possible. In most cases, the best ways you can do this are:

- Match your skills and abilities to those demanded by the job.
- Clearly spell out what those skills and abilities are at the very top of your resume.
- Back this up with evidence—your on-the-job achievements and accomplishments.

Keeping your resume "honest"

Remember that hiring managers are often in a hurry to get someone on the job. When they come across too many adjectives, or get a sense that the applicant is trying too hard to sound perfect (rather than communicating skills and qualifications), they may just assume you don't have the relevant skills. They'll go on to the next resume in the stack, and look for essential items.

If you find yourself embellishing too much, maybe you need to look closely at what your skills really are. When employers come across too many "fluff" words, such as "self-motivated," "computer literate," or "hard working" they may simply not read the Experience section at the top of your resume, and just quickly scan your jobs. Then all that expensive paper and typesetting was for nothing! That's why I always remind people that it's *content* that matters most.

There's another reason for leaving out the "fluff": If employers think you're trying to embellish too much in your writing, they may wonder, "What is this person trying to cover up? A lack of genuine skill? A rocky job history?"

Never lie on your resume. Someday your boss may ask you to do something you can't and there goes your credibility, and your job! You must be able to back up everything on your resume during an interview, so it's up to you to develop your most important and relevant skills in light of the work you're seeking, and that's much easier to do when you give yourself credit for your real talents, spell them out simply, and then position them to their best advantage.

Job Search Facts

Starting to feel underqualified? Don't worry, because here are four more reasons why your Experience section can be so helpful. According to a survey by the American Society of Training and Development, the top four qualities employers are looking for today are:

1. The ability to learn.
2. The ability to listen and convey information.
3. The ability to solve problems in innovative ways.
4. The knowledge of how to get things done.

Resume essentials

You've already gathered all the detail you'll need to begin writing your resume when you filled out the worksheets in the previous chapter. But before we begin, let's review the definitions and importance of all the different pieces of information your resume may include:

1. Name, address, phone number. Hard to believe, but I've actually received resumes without phone numbers! Needless to say, those applicants didn't get far with our company. Be sure you've listed your contact information correctly. Also, include an e-mail address if you have one.

2. Job titles. These can be changed to be understood by as many employers as possible. For instance: "Entry-level Landscaper" can simply be written as "Landscaper." Don't, however, give yourself a "promotion," listing a title that implies more responsibility than you actually had.

3. Company names and dates. Unless you've had four or five jobs shorter than one year and are writing a purely functional resume, include company names and the locations (city *and* state, unless they're local). Use months as well as years, or omit months if it helps you leave out jobs or cover your tracks, but be consistent! Notice different ways of listing dates throughout the resume samples in this book.

4. Job duties. Identify key duties in your jobs, but don't write a comprehensive job description! Instead, highlight your achievements and how you exceeded job expectations. Include part-time employment when it applies to the position desired. You may also include part-time jobs or volunteer work that shows initiative, self-motivation, leadership, organizational, or communication skills.

5. Licenses and certifications. Include, for example, insurance and real estate sales licenses in addition to other applicable credentials such as "HAZMAT-certified." Also include civil service or government grades and classifications when appropriate for the type of job you're seeking.

6. Education. List the highest level reached first. Avoid listing high school if you have a college degree. Education becomes less important as your hands-on work experience grows. Place your Education section following Employment when you have several years of applicable work history.

You may include college attendance and course completions even if no degree has been earned.

Additional professional training should be included, especially if this was sponsored by an employer; it shows the firm had confidence in your ability to learn and succeed. List which firms sponsored the seminars or college courses. You may also include whether you "self-funded" college costs, if there's space on the page.

If you're right out of school with no applicable work experience, present your education right after your Experience section.

7. Languages. Fluency in a foreign language may be extremely valuable on the job. List your level of proficiency: "Speak conversational French," "Fluent in Spanish," "Read and write Italian," "Familiar with Russian." These can be mentioned in a communications bullet in your Experience section, or near the bottom in a Personal section as shown in some of the resume samples in this book.

8. Professional memberships. You should list trade and professional groups if they're relevant to your future job. This demonstrates an active interest in industry developments and that you share ideas with others in your field. These affiliations can prove very valuable in your job search when you get to personal networking.

Eliminate from your resume...

1. Salary requirements/history. When employers want to know your salary requirements, they generally want to know if they can afford you—or how cheaply they can get you. They also want to make sure they don't end up paying more than they need to fill the position. If this is requested in the job posting or advertisement, you may include it, but on a separate "Salary History" sheet and never on the resume itself.

According to a survey of more than 200 employers who posted job openings stating, "Resumes without salary history will not be considered," more than 90 percent said they would *still* call a candidate if they thought they were right for the job, even if salary history or requirements were not included!

If salary information is not requested, then do not offer it; you could be knocked out of consideration for being over- or under-priced. Another option is to mention a salary range in a cover letter. ("I am seeking a salary between $30,000 and $37,000.") But be sure you state a range that you would be willing to accept. It's best, however, to avoid discussion of salary until you've hooked the employer—once you get an offer, *then* you can negotiate compensation.

2. "Resume" at the top of the page or "References Available Upon Request" at the end. If it's not clear that your resume's a resume, then it's time to do some major rewriting. As for references, create a separate References sheet, with three or four names, titles, and phone numbers of previous supervisors, if you are sure they will give you a positive reference. You should print these on the same paper stock as your resume. Bring this page, along with your resume, to complete the job application.

The personnel representative or hiring manager may want to call a former employer; usually someone will check with you before contacting your current employer. Double-check this at the interview if you are concerned about keeping your job search confidential.

3. Reasons for leaving a job. Never include this information on your resume—you want to highlight positives, not negatives. The only exception to this is if you were promoted or transferred within a company. Why? Because this shows continuity and growth—*positive* reasons. Even if your reasons for leaving a company are good (another company or headhunter sought you out and hired you away), you don't want a prospective employer focusing on this and wondering whether you'll be a loyal employee.

You may be asked why you left a particular position during the interview—and you should be prepared to answer these questions then. Rehearse a concise response with as positive a spin as possible.

4. Religious or political groups. This type of information has a chance of working against you, so don't offer it unless you know it will be perceived positively. Try to put business considerations first. What do these associations have to do with the position you're seeking? Like anything else, if it won't actually help you get in the door, leave it out.

If you have little or no job history, but lots of experience with churches, synagogues, schools, or service groups, (Kiwanis, Boy Scouts, etc.) then you should develop and include this experience on your resume. Extract your best communication, organizational and leadership skills used with these groups and paraphrase them in your Experience or Profile section.

5. Any negative information. Remember that to many employers, resume reading is a process of elimination, so you must not give the reader any reason to take you out of the running. Never mention lawsuits or a bad experience with a former supervisor, and avoid including any item that could be seen as affecting your performance on the job—for example, the fact that you were unemployed for two years because of an illness. True, this information may be disclosed to the employer at some point. But you don't have to "spill your guts" up front in your resume.

6. A photograph. Unless you're applying for a job as a model, don't include a picture or any other physical description of yourself. First, while it may be both illegal and unethical to select employees based on looks, if you provide a photo you open yourself up to being considered based on your appearance. Don't subject yourself to the personal biases of the HR department or hiring supervisor.

Optional items

1. Title. If you're applying at a large company that may be hiring for many positions at the same time, this component will help quickly match your position to the job you're seeking. If, however, you are *more* interested in getting hired by the company, and less interested in what job you are hired for, you might consider dropping the title.

2. Objective. This element helps define and summarize your job goals so that the reader can quickly determine what you're seeking. It also, however, focuses on what *you* want. That's fine, as long as you know for certain that what you want matches *exactly* with what the employer wants. Objectives are best when they're specific and focused rather than broad and vague.

3. Military service. You should include any positive experience in the military, especially technical skills acquired. If you're seeking a position with a firm involved in defense contracting that hires former military personnel, you may be just what they're looking for. Include highest rank attained, supervisory experience, and applicable training. For technical positions, include systems and equipment operated, repaired, or maintained.

If your only applicable work experience was in the military, then this must be developed like any other job. On the other hand, if you're looking for work that's completely unrelated to skills gained during your time in the military, you may only list highest rank attained, and city and state of deployment.

4. A "Personal" or "Interests" section. If you need to fill room at the bottom of the page, include two to three lines outlining your interests. But make sure the interests you choose match in some way the skills and responsibilities demanded by the job. For example, if you're applying for a job as a clerk in a fabric store, definitely add "sewing" as a hobby.

The interests you list may also represent *indirect* skills that may reflect positively on your potential. For example, playing on a recreational sports team may indicate that you work well with others—you're a "team" player. Your involvement in Big Brothers or Sisters shows you may be a good role model and have leadership potential.

Of course, omit items that have no connection to tackling the job—especially pastimes that might be considered controversial or in conflict with the job. (You're applying for a job at the humane society? Probably not a good idea to mention your passion for taxidermy.)

5. Age and marital status. Legally, these two items should have no bearing on whether you're called in for an interview. But let's face it, some employers still discriminate based on age and marital status. Revealing your age can label you as too young or too old. What if you're twice as old as the president of the company, or half as old as the average manager? You may be perfect for the job, but such prejudice can run deep. Leave out your age altogether, and get the reader to focus on your relevant skills and abilities.

Omit marital status, unless this will demonstrate a certain stability and improve your chances of getting an interview, or you are applying for a job that specifically requests a husband-and-wife team (cross-country truckers or bed-and-breakfast managers).

One page or two?

Contrary to popular belief, one page is not always best. Two-page resumes earned a bad reputation years ago because people were putting too much useless information in them. They were writing long, irrelevant job histories or expanding too much on their personal likes and dislikes, hobbies, and so on.

Try to think in terms of *relevance* rather than number of pages. We write plenty of two-page resumes for our clients. Unless you have an extensive *and relevant* work history, or a detailed technical background of more than five years, try to keep your resume to one page—but don't leave out important skills simply to *force* your resume onto one page!

Remember, what counts most is the *content* of your resume. So think in terms of an advertisement. You want to grab your reader's attention by highlighting the benefits that your experience and skills will bring to the position. Whether that takes one page or two depends upon how many *benefits* you have to offer.

Pack Action Into Your Resume

To pack the most punch into your resume, remember to think like an advertiser. Use language and words that add strength to your descriptions of your work experience, skills, and training. As the Madison Avenue types would say, "Make it sizzle!" True, your statements and listings will tend to be written in short, brief, and succinct phrases. But that doesn't mean they have to be boring or "passive."

Professional Writer's Tip

It's okay to use sentences that take "I," "we," "he," "she," and other pronouns for granted. Omit these words altogether. Use the abbreviated third-person form shown in the Experience sections in this book. This is more direct. It helps you get straight to your qualifications and *sell* them. When space is tight, however, or if you must have all of your qualifications on one page, you can reduce the Experience section to one or two short paragraphs with bullets.

Go for strong, action-oriented words when describing your experiences. Avoid passive-sounding verbs such as "did," "was," and "used." And employ more powerful descriptors like "exceeded," "increased," "accomplished," and "directed" as they fit. Try to vary the use of the words you choose; while "achieved" is a terrific word to describe your accomplishments on the job, it loses its impact if you repeat it in each bulleted listing.

When developing your resume, keep a dictionary and perhaps a thesaurus by your side. A thesaurus will help you find synonyms for commonly used words when you're searching for a fresh way to describe a similar experience.

For a quick reference, the following list features some powerful, high-impact words you might find helpful when writing your resume.

Power words

Here's a sample of powerful, high impact words:

Achieved	Demonstrated	Introduced	Reinforced
Adapted	Designed	Investigated	Reorganized
Administered	Developed	Maintained	Researched
Advised	Drafted	Managed	Restructured
Amended	Eliminated	Modified	Reversed
Analyzed	Established	Monitored	Reviewed
Approved	Evaluated	Motivated	Revised
Assigned	Expanded	Organized	Saved
Assisted	Expedited	Participated	Scheduled
Budgeted	Focused	Performed	Screened
Built	Forecasted	Planned	Solved
Collected	Formulated	Prepared	Spearheaded
Compiled	Generated	Processed	Streamlined
Computed	Guided	Produced	Strengthened
Conducted	Implemented	Promoted	Structured
Controlled	Improved	Proposed	Supervised
Coordinated	Increased	Provided	Supported
Created	Initiated	Purchased	Taught
Cut	Innovated	Recommended	Trained
Decreased	Instituted	Recruited	Trimmed
Delegated	Interpreted	Reduced	Updated

Is a Title Or Objective For You?

Resume-writing professionals argue about the value of including job objectives or job titles in resumes. Some claim that the two elements are unnecessary and just take up space. Others believe such components add focus to the resume, and quickly tell a busy employer exactly what position the applicant is interested in. First, let's define each element, and then examine its merits and weaknesses.

The Title

The more straightforward of the two elements is the Title, and its purpose is pretty self-explanatory. It's simply two or three words that define the position you're applying for, centered at the top of your resume, and typically presented in all-cap treatment.

The Title is helpful in telling the busy resume screener exactly what position you are interested in. It's best to use a title when you are applying for a specific job opening—and in this case, it's essential that the title be exactly as it was presented in the want ad or job posting that you're responding to. In previous jobs, you may have been called a line supervisor, but if the position was advertised as the "Production Team Captain," *that's* what you want to put down as the title.

If, however, you are merely interested in working for this company in any capacity, and would be interested in other job openings, then you may not want to limit yourself to the one job title. In that case, consider leaving off the Title, and address your overall interest in the company in the cover letter.

The Title is easily changed with every resume you send out, and should be tailored to suit the job opening. Examples include:

- Carpentry/Construction
- Production Management
- Mechanic: Production Equipment
- Warehousing / Distribution
- Route Driver

The Objective

An Objective is simply a short statement that describes the job *you want*. It appears at the top of the resume, directly after your name and contact information.

Now, as you read this definition, you may already see what the weakness of such a statement might be. Remember what we've said about the purpose of a resume? How it's supposed to focus on what the prospective employer wants? But the Objective focuses on what *you* want!

I believe, however, that there are times when the Objective can enhance your resume. For example, if you know exactly what you want to do and your job goal matches perfectly with the job you're applying for, then, by all means, introduce your resume with a targeted Objective that zeroes in on the job.

An Objective may also be important if your current job goal doesn't exactly match your past experience. Perhaps your past three jobs have been in retail sales, but you're applying for a position as a day-care worker. Without an Objective at the top of your resume, the resume screener may discard your resume as he or she scans your experience and doesn't see a connection.

However, if you're not exactly sure about the job responsibilities of the position you're applying for—or you're applying at a company where you'd be willing to consider other openings just to get in, then don't waste resume space by including an Objective.

Because it's so important that the Objective and prospective job responsibilities jibe, it's best to customize the Objective for each resume you send. This will be easy if you are creating your resume on computer.

The best Objectives are specific, including a job title and indicating clear focus. Here are some examples:

OBJECTIVE: Quality Control Supervisor. A position where profit-building skills would be utilized.

OBJECTIVE: A position in Shipping and Receiving, where proven abilities in packing, distribution, and accurate record-keeping would be of value.

OBJECTIVE: A position utilizing 11 years in construction (or plant) operations, where a strict attention to detail (or profitability) would be of value.

Because a company may be hiring for many different positions, an Objective or Title will quickly help the reader understand what job you're shooting for. If you are interested in a broad range of jobs within a given company, you may consider omitting these components. If so, make sure you use a combination format, and that the first Experience bullet gives the reader a big picture of the type of skills and knowledge you offer. This puts additional importance on the Experience section of your resume. For advice on building this section, read on.

Experience: Showcase Your Skills

The Experience section appears at the beginning of the resume, immediately following the name and contact information, and Objective or Title, if one is used. Its purpose is to offer the reader a quick summary of your key qualifications and achievements. It gives you the opportunity to sell your skills in a glance to the reader.

Typically, the Experience section is a key component of the functional format or the combination format, where other sections, such as Employment or Education serve to support it with detail. But you might also include a shorter Experience section at the top of a chronological format, where it provides a nice highlight and summary of your work experience and training.

Even though the Experience section may focus on work history, you may also add to it skills and achievements gathered in nonpaid positions, as well as education and training. This is an excellent opportunity to translate *all* your skills and experiences into job-related abilities.

Some people think it's enough to list their jobs. But when you sift through your transferable skills and spell them out for the reader, right on top or your resume, you'll always have a better chance of getting your foot in the door. With a strong summary, you're in charge of what you want the employer to know about you. And your work history will follow this section, to support your statements with evidence and detail.

Here's an example of how effective this skills summary can be: I once wrote a short Experience section—only six lines of text—for a new college graduate. He sent out 20 resumes and received four job offers in just the first two weeks! (See Larry Capp's *Graduate* resume, on page 196).

The Experience section gives you control over what direction to market yourself: what skills to emphasize, what skills to downplay, and what key words to include. Without it, you're at the mercy of your job history.

Your Experience section may contain marketable skills and abilities, *whether or not you've used them on the job.* Spell out your most relevant skills and abilities, regardless of where you learned those skills. You can list just about any skill, aptitude, or training with the right qualifying words. Start with the skills you deem to be most relevant and, thus, most valued by the prospective employer—*and* that are your strongest.

Use data from the worksheets in Chapter 1 and think about how to best extract and present your skills and abilities from you actual work experience and training.

This section should be kept to one to three bulleted paragraphs for a one-page resume, and two to five bulleted paragraphs for a two-page resume. You might also consider calling this section Profile, Summary of Experience, or simply Summary.

Professional Writer's Tip

The very first bullet or paragraph of your Experience section should act as an umbrella over all the rest of the items and give the reader a "big picture" of where you're coming from and what type of strengths and abilities you will bring to the new position.

Begin the Experience section with just a few words about the types of skills you have that would best match the job. These might be communication skills, (written, speaking, reporting, or creating graphs and charts), or analytical skills (production line setup, systems, or familiarity with specific equipment).

Here's a list of sentence starters:

- Proficient in...
- Experience in...
- Skilled in...
- Perform...
- Plan and implement...
- Utilize...
- Familiar with...

- Comprehensive experience in...
- Extensive knowledge of...
- Proven abilities in..
- Plan and conduct...
- Train and supervise staff in...
- Knowledge of...
- Trained in...

Think about how your qualifications can be shaped into phrases your prospective boss would appreciate. Write down everything you think of, then narrow it down and make a short list of those items you feel are most applicable to the desired position.

Keep it relevant

The main goal here is to keep your Experience section relevant to both your needs and the employers. This section is about overall ability. A trainee, intern, or new entrant into the job market may have many abilities and very little work history. We've found that one of best ways to get someone in the door for an interview is to market all of his or her relevant ability.

If you're still having trouble starting this section, simply think of the *type* of work you've done that would be useful or relevant, or shows an *aptitude* for the next job—then extract those skills and develop them. Here are some examples:

- Skilled in the repair and maintenance of mechanical (or electrical) systems, including pumps and conveyors.
- Assist in report preparation and analysis, data compilation, and review.
- Plan and conduct written and oral presentations in a professional manner for work crews and supervisors.

This, combined with your education and knowledge of the field, will all help project you as able to walk in, tackle the responsibilities and succeed in your new job.

Group similar skills together

When you have more than a few skills to highlight, always try to group like skills together. Following are examples of bullet points for the Experience section, organized into skills sets. Notice how each paragraph attempts to build on the previous one. You may use such groupings as:

Mechanical skills:

- Skilled in the setup, repair, and daily maintenance of production, packaging, and product testing equipment.
- Strong aptitude in the repair and maintenance of mechanical systems, including industrial packaging and CNC manufacturing equipment.
- Comprehensive experience as Journeyman Carpenter, including rough frame/trim work and quality control for custom-built homes and commercial structures.
- Trained in the operation and repair of punch presses, slitters, shrink wrappers, and conveyor systems.

Here's another example of an Experience section. Have you ever helped train, supervise, motivate, or simply orient or coordinate production staff? If so, your next bullet in the Experience section may use some or all of the following items:

Training skills:

- Assist in staff training and supervision in production line setup, assembly operations, quality control, packing, and shipping.
- Skilled in group and individual training of work crews and support staff (and/or supervisors), with full responsibility for the design of training and performance testing programs.

In all cases, try to avoid overused, general statements such as, "Excellent communication skills" and instead give the reader specifics. Without details and examples, your statements could read as "fluff." For instance, in the following example, the writer offers specific applications for good communication skills, both written and oral:

Communication skills:

- Plan and conduct written and oral presentations in a professional manner.
- Assist in staff training, performance reviews, and written documentation. Compile and present status reports to management on production activities.
- Closely monitor and report on quantities, parts, components, component/finished good prices, labor cost, and quality levels.

Whether your Experience section becomes the backbone of your resume, or you use it as an opportunity to summarize and showcase your strengths, this section will be key in communicating quickly to the reader that you are a candidate worth getting to know better. Take the time to carefully craft your Experience section. The payoff will be truly worthwhile.

Employment: Build an Impressive History

Traditionally, the Employment section has been the heart of the resume. In the chronological format, it comes up front in the resume, following the name and contact information, and the Objective or Title, if used.

In the functional resume, however, the Employment section may be absent, replaced by an expanded Experience section, which highlights and summarizes experience and duties. Most often, a combination format will include the Employment section, following a more beefed-up Experience section.

In any case, this section is one of the more "structured" elements of the resume. This is where you tell the reader what you've done or achieved at other companies. Here's where you back up and verify the statements about skills and abilities in your Experience or Summary section. Almost always, your previous jobs are listed in reverse chronological order—that is, your most recent work experience is listed first, followed by the previous job, and so forth.

Each separate job listing in your Employment section will include the following components:

Company name. Use the complete name, avoiding nicknames or abbreviations that may not be familiar to the reader.

Company location. Use city and state only, and don't list the company phone number—you want the employer to call *you* first.

Your job title. You might consider "translating" your title to a more universal title if the internal label is unusual or unfamiliar to other work environments. Just don't "promote" yourself to a job level you didn't really have.

Dates of employment. Use year *and* month. However, you may omit the month, particularly if you have a history of longevity—staying with employers for many years. In this case, as long as the years are correct for the jobs you're listing, you could leave out irrelevant jobs lasting only a few months.

Brief job description. Don't take a lot of space to do this. One or two sentences should be enough to give the reader a general idea of what you do. Also, chances are the prospective employer has a good idea of what the job involves, especially if you're applying for the same type of position.

Try to include specifics, though. For example, if you supervise people as part of your responsibilities, indicate how many employees report to you. If you're in charge of a budget, include the amount. And if there is anything unique or unusual about the job—that the title or general description doesn't reveal—be sure to mention that, as well. For example: "Travel to offices in Mexico six times a year."

Achievements at each position. Here's where you get to brag a little. Employers love to see achievements, accomplishments, and results that demonstrate excellence on the job. Here you can list awards and what they were for. Typically, this information will appear in a list or bullet format, which helps set off and draw the reader's eye to it.

- Ranked #1 in quality control among 18 QC representatives and earned a vacation to Hawaii.
- Increased this department's profit margin from 18% to 21%.

Check the resumes in this book—they're loaded with achievements and quantifiable, verifiable results. Did you increase the efficiency of operations? Reduce downtime? Speed turnaround or inventory turns? How much money did you save the company by introducing a new maintenance procedure, system, operation, or piece of equipment?

Try to give the reader a scope and perspective to understand your achievements: What percentage of overall revenues? How many others were you competing with for the top sales award? Do this without misrepresenting yourself and without using generic language or vague wording like "excellent communication skills," "self-motivated," or "computer literate."

When you proofread your resume, ask yourself whether your descriptions of achievements could apply to just anyone—or uniquely yourself. Step back and look deeper into your skill sets. What *measurable* results did you bring about in your previous jobs—in terms of dollars saved or earned, time saved, or production increased?

Think about what you really mean by phrases such as "excellent communication skills," for example. Does that mean you can research and write (or produce) status reports for staff and management? If so, on what subjects or topics: product or material costs, finished goods, labor costs or quality? And how did you perform them in your previous job? Did you win awards? Get promotions? Improve conditions?

If you find yourself trying to stretch the truth, then maybe you're not right for the position you're shooting for. It's time to reassess, and look at yourself more objectively.

Are your talents transferable to other fields or markets? Someone with strong mechanical skills should be able to learn how to repair and maintain different types of equipment.

Following are two examples of high-impact job descriptions. Note the overall layout, including placement of dates off to the right (to de-emphasize) and the company name emphasized with an underline. This emphasis creates an "umbrella" effect over the job title and description. Also note that the bullets are used sparingly and only for emphasis of various key achievements. In addition, the first sentence gives an overall, *big picture* description of daily duties. Following is a breakdown of specific duties.

EMPLOYMENT: <u>Mitsubishi Semiconductor America, Inc.</u>, Durham, NC   1/85-3/99
Quality Assurance Operations / Test Production
Performed functional, electrical, in-process and final inspections on a wide range of semiconductor materials and devices. Responsible for detailed, quality-level checks and visual audits on module, assembled and test devices during various production processes. Conducted group and individual training for up to 16 workers in all production line testing and quality control procedures.
- Trained on statistical process control and electro-static discharge.
- Operated x-ray machines, microscopes, digital calipers, component testers, lead bend machines, as well as tape and reel for discreet devices and Topaz soldering equipment for PC boards.
- Directly involved in packaging, assembly lines and topaz line procedures; utilized acoustic and other precision measurement instruments in a class-10 clean-room environment.

In the next example, the applicant had originally supplied a vague description—something like "Level I Shop Assistant." So I changed it to something more descriptive, to give the reader a better sense of what the individual did.

EMPLOYMENT: Dreisilker Electrical Motors, Glen Ellyn, IL   7/76–present
Shop Repair and Maintenance
Responsible for training and supervising up to 4 in all shop procedures, including the complete teardown, repair, assembly and test running of electrical motors. Gained extensive skills with a wide range of equipment, including the troubleshooting and maintenance of:
- Sleeve and ball-bearing motors up to 5,000 h.p.
- Medium and large generators, slip-ring motors, vertical high thrust hollow shaft pump motors.
- AC and DC motors up to 5,000 h.p.
- Medium and large induction synchronous motors, as well as eddy current clutch motors.
▸ Repair special grinder and hermetic motors, including removing stators and installing medium and large vertical motor thrust pumps.
- Install and braze rotor bars and connect end rings.
- Inspect and measure shafts and bearing housings.
- Produce status reports for management.

Remember that bullets add white space, give the eye a focal point, and help break up gray blocks of type. Avoid repeating specifics that already appear in the Experience or Profile section. In the Employment section, you should be concentrating on specific achievements, measured as much as possible in terms such as dollars, percentages, and numbers. For example, if you helped revise a procedure that saved the company time or money, indicate how many hours, days, or months, and dollars or percentages.

A note about dates: If you've been working for a long time, we sometimes recommend moving job experiences that occurred 18 or more years ago into a section labeled "Prior Experience." Of course, an employer will be most interested in your most recent experience; particularly if your "ancient" work history is irrelevant or adds nothing to your credentials, you may want to leave it off entirely. But if those experiences do enhance your overall value, you can still mention them, but minimize them so you have space to focus on your current experiences.

Your employment history isn't the only measure of your experience that prospective employers will want to know about. They'll also need to know about your education, special training, certifications, and other credentials that provided you with the skills and knowledge you need for your job. The Education section will be explored in the next chapter.

Education: Play Up Your Strongest Credentials

How should you list your formal education, training, special courses, and required certifications? This all depends on relevance. Remember, your resume is your "advertisement" or your marketing instrument; you want to *lead* with the information that will put you in the best light, that will play up your strengths. So, if your education is your strongest suit, put them at the beginning of your resume.

For example, perhaps you are applying for a job as a photographer's assistant. If all your work experience has been in retail sales, but you recently completed several photography courses, you'll want to list your Education section before your Employment section.

For most of us, however, our work history may be more relevant or recent that our educational particulars. That's why you'll see that most resumes include the Education section toward the end of the resume.

Following are a couple of examples of Education sections I developed for clients. Note that the layout is consistent with the

Employment sections illustrated in the previous chapter. Whatever format you choose to present your work history and education in, you should be consistent from section to section.

EDUCATION: Judson College, Elgin, IL
Associate Degree: Electrical Systems   Graduated 12/98
Successful completion of courses in electrical system configuration, wiring, industrial fuse-box installation, line testing and troubleshooting.

Elgin Community College, Elgin, IL   Spring, 1995
Completed various liberal arts courses.

Grand Canyon University, Phoenix, AZ   Fall, 1994
Completed one year's studies in liberal arts.

If you have not earned a degree, it will still be to your advantage to indicate that you have or are taking courses, even listing the specific classes that may be relevant to your job goals.

EDUCATION: Bergen Community College, Paramus, NJ   1/93
Completed courses related to Business Management

Plaza School of Technology, Paramus, NJ   7/92
Trained in CAD versions 11 and 12 (Computer-Aided Drafting.)

National Education Center, Rets Campus, Nutley, NJ   4/90
Associate Degree: Electronics Engineering Technology

CERTIFICATE: HAZMAT Certified by the State of Illinois,   1999

Some clients ask me, "Should I include my high school information?" I tell them yes if there's no other indication that you have graduated from high school. In other words, if you list that you've earned a bachelor's degree or associate's degree, it will be assumed that you graduated from high school. Without this additional educational experience, you are wisest to add that you graduated from high school.

As for dates, I sometimes advise leaving off date of graduation—whether for high school or college. Sadly, age discrimination still exists and often older workers are the targets of this bias. But remember, if you omit the dates for one listing, you really must leave them off for all.

For example, if you choose to list that you earned an associate's degree, but leave off the fact that you did so in 1962, then you should also leave off the date for your recent completion of a certification program. (In this case, it's probably better to leave off the associate's degree entirely—it's not likely to add much value if you've gathered years of work experience in between.)

I recommend listing certifications and training programs following formal education listings such as high school and college. But I also would mention the most relevant certifications in the Experience or Profile section at the top of the resume.

Especially if you have a minimal amount of formal education, your certifications, as well as workshops, seminars, and other professional training experiences you've gathered become more important. When you list these, be sure to point out any pertinent subjects covered in the training, and make note that you "completed" or "graduated" from the course.

EDUCATION: Successful completion of a CAD/CAM seminar by Hewlett Packard Corporation.
Completed seminars by Anthony Robbins and Zig Ziglar on communication, sales and self-motivation.

Always give yourself credit for any kind of training, formal or informal. This communicates a lot more than the fact that you have acquired a certain knowledge. It also conveys to the reader that you are self-motivated, have a desire to learn more about your field or industry, and that you want to grow and advance—traits that all savvy employers are looking for.

Design Your Eye-catching Resume

The "look" of your resume may be as important as the content—at least in the first few seconds when it must grab the reader's attention. Your resume must appear flawless—this marks you as a professional who is attentive to detail. A clean, light look is ideal, because it gives the impression that your resume will be easy to read and extract important information.

You can achieve this appealing look through the effective use of a variety of elements, including type (size and style), white space, margins, and special treatments such as bullets, indenting, and boldface type. And you can enhance the overall appearance of your resume by *how* you create it (whether on computer or typewriter) and how you print it.

Computer, typewriter, or professional typesetter?

Your first decision is to determine how you'll create your resume. On your old manual typewriter? On the neighbor's computer? Or perhaps you're a two-finger typist and would rather write something longhand and have a professional design and typeset the information.

Of course, if you put yourself in the hands of a professional resume writer, this will be your easiest course of action. But if you want to develop your own resume, I recommend you use a computer. Not only will you be able to get a much more professional look, you'll have a greater choice of type styles and design elements so that you can create a more readable look than you could with a typewriter. You'll also be able to store your resume, modify it, update it—and customize it with each job you apply for.

If you don't have a computer, there are plenty of options for finding one. Most libraries offer computer use to the public, not to mention schools and business centers such as Kinko's.

You may own or have access to one of the newer typewriters that features boldfacing, changeable print wheels, and lift-off correction. The reproduction quality of masters printed on some of these models rivals that of laser printers and typesetting. Although this won't provide you with the storing and customizing benefits of a computer, you can create an excellent resume master and have it reproduced on a high-quality photocopier—resulting in a very professional-looking resume.

What type face? What size?

Type faces used for text are either *serif* or *sans serif*. Serifs are the "hands" and "feet" at the top and bottom of letters. Serif type faces, then, are fonts such as the one you're reading now that have such "hands" and "feet." Sans serif type faces utilize letters without these flourishes.

This is an example of a sans serif type face.

Which should you use? Serif types are recommended for most printed materials. Just about every major newspaper uses serif type. Why? Serif is easy to read. The theory is that the serifs help the eye move along from word to word more easily. If you are in a creative or high-tech field such as graphic arts or design, or your resume copy is pretty spare, you might consider a sans serif face such as Helvetica, Kent, or New Gothic.

Keep your type size between 10 and 12 points—11-point type is best. Anything smaller is hard for the eye to scan and anything bigger can seem excessive. Fill the page with essential information, *then* adjust the size of type and the margins and tabs to make it all fit!

Bullet points and white space

One of the best ways to make your resume attractive and readable is to use "white space." Break up blocks of text and add white space to your resume with bulleted text and healthy margins and indents. This helps make the highlights of your background stand out, while giving the eye a focal point.

We usually indent (tab) after each bullet. There are many different types of bullets—especially if you are able to use a computer to design your resume.

Another way to add white space is to use a return at the end of every sentence, and to add blank spaces between groups of text. There are plenty of samples of use of white space in the following resume examples.

Yet another method of adding white space, used in just about every resume in this book, is to indent each paragraph after the appropriate heading (such as Experience, Employment, and so on). I prefer an indent of 1.5 to 2 inches.

EXPERIENCE:
- Extensive background in the assembly and installation of electrical components and machine parts, on job sites and production lines.
- Skilled in troubleshooting and promptly taking corrective action; read and interpret blueprints, and bills of materials; adhere to safety policies, procedures and codes.
- Utilize ARC and MIG welders, micrometers, air gun nailers, torque wrenches, hammers, screwdrivers, drill presses, shears, and Whitney presses; operate forklifts and cranes.

You may also use a simple dash or asterisk, but as you can see, these don't stand out as well as the computer-generated bullets:

* Skilled in the total rebuilding and fabrication of custom and stock engines, differentials and gears, as well as blown gas and alcohol motors.
- Proficient in boring and honing blocks and heads; skilled in the use of lathes, mills, grinders, and all general shop equipment.

Use "frills" such as boldfacing, underlining, italics, bullets, or dashes only now and then, and not on every line. These graphics lose their impact when they're overused. They should only be used to make major points stand out, or to set items apart and break up type. Avoid using all the elements—boldfacing, underlining, or italics—in the same resume. Choose a combination of any *two*. My personal favorites are bolding and underlining, but pick whichever you like.

Some of these techniques may seem trivial, but it's the minor details that make up a great resume. Without attention to detail, you end up with yet another data-sheet resume that won't work very well. The techniques presented here will distance you from the pack and help you win the resume game.

Line length

The resumes I design for my clients follow a simple format. The body copy is usually indented about 1.5 inches from the left margin. This allows for shorter lines and makes the resume more scannable to the eye. This also gives greater white space and an excellent place to put your section headings (Objective and Experience, for example). Margins should be 1 inch all around, but they may be shortened to .75 inch or widened up to 1.5 inches as needed to fit your information on one or two pages. Again, don't be afraid to use two pages if that's what it takes to develop and market your skills!

If you still need more or less space than margin shifting allows, change your type size by one-half point, but try to keep it around 11 points.

Avoid violating your margins or hyphenating words at the end of a line. However, you can make an exception to this rule for compound words such as self-employed, when the line ends after "self."

Don't worry about squaring off (full justifying) your lines unless space is really tight. Many resumes in this guide are fully justified, in order to pack more information on each page, but notice that we almost always place a return at the end of each individual sentence. This automatically adds white space between lines and your resume avoids that "tombstone" look, with big blocks of gray type.

Placement of dates

I recommend placement of dates directly across from job title or company name, flush right. An assistant director for alumni career services at a major university said she liked to see dates placed immediately after the company location: "Chicago, IL, 8/93-1/94." I agree with this if you'd like to hide or mask dates of shorter positions.

Printing your resume

If you're creating your resume on a computer, chances are you have access to a printer that will produce a good-quality copy—or copies—as you need them. Be sure the printer is a laser or inkjet printer—never use a dot matrix printer, as this will produce a copy that's difficult to read and not professional-looking.

As for photocopying your resume, remember that no copy machine can reproduce the print quality of a genuine laser-typeset original. Avoid photocopying more than 12 resumes at a time.

If you don't anticipate wanting to customize your resume for different job opportunities, visit a Kinko's or the copy department of a major office supplies store. These establishments use high-quality photocopiers. You can typically choose to do it yourself or have it done for you. Either way, run a sample before you print the entire order—you want to make sure there are no damages to the printer, which may show up as black or gray streaks, or spots on your resume. This will also give you a chance to adjust the lightness or darkness of the printer.

What color paper?

I advise my clients to stick to white, off-white, or ivory colors of paper—these are good, easy-to-read colors. Avoid grays or beiges as they reduce contrast between paper and ink. Lighter paper works much better when your resume is faxed to an employer or scanned into a database. Also avoid the splotchy parchment papers, or those with unusual textures. If you want your resume to stand out on a desk of white papers, use a natural or ivory color. Check the linen designs such as Classic Linen Avon Brilliant White or a smoother paper, such as Strathmore, available in white or natural colors.

The professionals I write for receive actual laser prints of their resume on their choice of paper (I usually recommend white linen). I can also provide them with a laser master on plain white paper to use for economical photocopying at a good quick-print shop, or they can get more laser prints on top-grade paper at three for $1.

Proofread, Proofread, Proofread!

Before printing or sending out a single resume, always proofread it slowly and carefully. Check *everything*, including dates of employment, the spelling of company names and your name and address. One trick that helps catch typos is reading your resume backwards. Start with the very last word and read to the first. This forces you to focus on the words individually. Have relatives and friends read over your resume, too. After all, you may be too close to it to catch errors that may be obvious to a more objective reader.

You'd be surprised what can slip by in the finished version. This is your life, your career, your future on paper—it must be as close to perfect as possible!

————————————————

Chapter 9

Are Electronic Resumes the Way of the future?

Your resume may very well be viewed by an HR representative, and then perhaps by the hiring manager. But to save time, a growing number of companies are using computers to scan and sort through the hundreds, or even thousands of resumes they may receive. Two such companies that use computers to scan resumes in the Midwest are Motorola and First Card, one of the largest credit card processing companies.

Your resume may be placed on a scanner and loaded onto a large computer database. When this happens, your document is now an electronic—or digital—resume. Employers can then use special software to find certain "keywords" for a match.

Examples of keywords may include types of computer software such as:

Windows 98	Macintosh
QuarkXpress	Lotus
MS Office	PowerPoint

Keywords may include operational skills such as:

Accounts payable   Payroll processing

Inventory control

Keywords may include industry-specific terms such as:

Automotive   Electronics

Food and beverage   Carpentry

Mechanic

Or keywords may identify the level of employment such as:

Manager   Supervisor

Executive   Assistant

Entry-level   Intern

Formatting tips for electronic resumes

Of course, nothing is perfect, and that holds true for document scanners. If your resume is scanned from paper into a computer system, letters and sometimes entire words may be read incorrectly. Underlining, italics, and certain type faces can be misinterpreted, and essential keywords may not be picked up by the computer system.

The best way around this problem is to bypass the paper scanning procedure and *e-mail* your resume directly to the employer. That way, the resume is already digital, and there's very little chance of words being misread. You may include a disk with your resume, but make sure you also send a paper version, in case the recipient doesn't take the time to copy your resume from disk.

Of course, many of the guidelines for designing traditional paper resumes (discussed in Chapter 8) will not apply to preparing an electronic resume.

Wayne M. Gonyea is an electronic career strategist and developer of numerous career-related Web sites, including Career and Resume Management for the 21st Century! (crm21.com). He is co-author of *Electronic Resumes* and *Selling on the Internet*, and a member of PARW, NRWA, and holds a masters degree in counseling. His e-mail address is: online@resumexpress.com. Mr. Gonyea offers the following perspective and advice regarding electronic resumes.

Electronic Resumes,
The Wave of the Future:
by Wayne Gonyea

Computer scanning is requiring a major re-engineering of the concept and process of using resumes for job hunting.

OnLine Solutions, Inc., emphasizes the importance of OCR (Optical Character Recognition) in the entire process. OCR comes into play initially when the paper resume is scanned into computers. Although resumes can be received by companies electronically via e-mail and diskette, many of them are still received on paper, thus requiring scanning.

Resume management systems scan resumes into databases, search the databases on command, and rank the resumes according to the number of resulting "hits" they receive. At times, such searches utilize multiple (10 to 20) criteria. Such resume management systems are usually utilized by major corporations and recruitment firms. The reliance upon resume management systems, coupled with the downsizing of human resource departments in many corporations, has resulted in a situation whereby many resumes are never seen by human eyes once they enter the electronic systems!

The lesson is to make your resume as computer- and scanner-friendly as possible so that its life in a database will be extended and its likelihood of producing "hits" is enhanced.

In order to satisfy the idiosyncrasies of the scanning process, a new resume style using "keywords," has developed. Keywords refer to those words or phrases used for searches of databases for resumes that match. This match is called a "hit" and occurs when one or more resumes are selected as matching the various criteria (keywords) used in the search.

Keywords tend to be more of the noun or noun-phrase type (Total Quality Management, UNIX, Bio-Chemist) as opposed to power action verbs often found in traditional resumes (developed, coordinated, empowered, organized).

Another way to look at keyword phrases is to think in terms of job duties. Detailing your job duties may require a modified mindset for those of you accustomed to traditional resume writing. However, the words and phrases that detail your job duties are the phrases—the keywords—that provide your resume with "hits."

Note that the keyword resume must contain an adequate description of the job-seeker's characteristics and industry-specific experience presented in keyword terms in order to accommodate the electronic/computer search process. These are the words and phrases that employers and recruiters use to search the databases for "hits"!

Use the following guidelines to enhance the processing of keyword resumes through the electronic system:

- Left-justify the entire document.
- Utilize a sans serif font (such as Arial or Helvetica) in 10-point type size.
- Avoid tabs.

- Avoid hard returns whenever possible.
- Avoid italic text, script, underlining, graphics, bold, and shading.
- Avoid horizontal and vertical lines.
- Avoid parentheses and brackets.
- Avoid compressed lines of print (typesetting and proportional spacing may cram too much into one line if there's a long word near the end of the sentence).
- Avoid faxed copies, which become fuzzy.

I suggest that successful job-seekers prepare two versions of their resume. The traditional market-driven resumes will continue to be designed for the eyes of "real people," to be viewed in "20 seconds or less," and follow the various formats presented by resume writers and resume-writing programs.

The keyword resume, however, should be developed, added to the successful job-seeker's arsenal, and utilized in any situation where computer scanning might possibly be involved.

Most employers are changing the way they use and retrieve information. Electronic scanning into databases using the Information Superhighway is the "way of the future."

Having noted Mr. Gonyea's valuable advice, take a look at this survey:

Job Search Facts

An OfficeTeam survey of 150 executives who responded from the nation's largest 1,000 companies found that they would prefer to get your resume the old-fashioned way, through the mail. That method ranked first at 21 percent, while fax and e-mail lagged far behind at 8 percent and 4 percent respectively. On the other hand, some companies prefer to receive resumes by fax or e-mail, as this speeds the process—you may jump ahead of the crowd if you can deliver your resume the same day, or the day after a job posting.

Diane Domeyer, executive director of OfficeTeam, commented on her preference for traditional paper resumes received in the mail: "It shows a candidate has extended a greater effort to personalize the information. In addition, such elements as the choice of paper, quality of printing, and layout of the document give insight to overall professionalism."

So what should you do? If you create and store your resume on computer, you'll have a little more flexibility. If you wish to send your resume via e-mail because you know a particular employer prefers to receive and store resumes electronically, then you can modify your "basic" resume as recommended by Mr. Gonyea. Save this as a *text only* file, and keep it as a separate file in your computer. When you want to respond to different job openings via e-mail, you can modify, cut, and paste into an e-mail and send it simply and quickly.

Notice that you shouldn't need to *attach* your resume file (which may convert it into some incompatible form for the recipient). By including it as part of the e-mail, you increase the likelihood that the resume will arrive intact and readable. Remember, though, that you can only use this cut-and-paste technique with a *text only* file.

The majority of employers still read the resumes they receive, so you're safe in sending a paper resume in most cases. When you do, just be sure to send it unfolded, with a cover letter, in a 9 x 12 envelope so that it arrives flat and neat. (Besides, most people grab the largest pieces of mail first—don't you?)

Now that your resume has been created, you need a solid plan, a job-hunting strategy that will allow you to maximize all that great information your resume contains. And that's what the next two chapters are all about.

————————————————

Chapter 10

Your Job Search
And the Role of
Your Resume

Perhaps you're at the beginning of your job search. You may have been laid off. Maybe you're doing fine at your current job, but you want more challenge, a better salary, or a new direction. Whatever your reasons for seeking a new job, you've got some challenges ahead of you. Job-hunting can be hard work, but the payoffs are well-worth it. And the good news is that now you have developed the most important tool in your job-hunting arsenal—your resume.

Now, your next step is to seek out those job opportunities! There's a world of possibility out there, and you want to explore every avenue in search of your ideal job. So where do you find out about job openings? Let's consider these options:

Your current employer

If you're lucky, your next great job could be with the company you're now working for. Most companies have a human resources department that posts job openings. Typically, current employees are given priority consideration for such positions. Often, the jobs are posted to employees before they are advertised in the want ads.

————————

And so, you have a leg up on the competition! You have a chance to get your resume in and schedule an interview *before* the deluge of interviews and responses starts coming in through the mail, fax, and computer.

Keep an eye out for such job postings, but go further in your search for internal opportunities. Talk to co-workers in other departments to learn about upcoming changes and expansions. Seek out opportunities to work on interdepartmental projects that put you in contact with *other* supervisors and managers. You'll be in a better position, then, when an opening comes up.

Your company's competitors

What better place to find job openings for positions that reflect your experience and skills than other companies *just like* the one you work for? In most cases, these other companies will be considered "the competition" for your current employer. Unless you have signed some sort of agreement not to work for a competitor within a period of time after you leave your company, these companies are great sources of job opportunities.

How to find out about them? You may belong to a trade organization where you meet with employees from such companies. Include some of these individuals in your "network" and touch base with them regularly to learn of opportunities.

You can also research opportunities at other companies through the Internet (even medium-sized and small companies often have Web sites that offer information and post job openings), and resources found in the reference section of any public library.

Trade or industry organizations

Such groups may be organized on a national or local level. There are opportunities for regular meetings and special events, where you can meet and "network" with other individuals. Most organizations have regularly published newsletters or magazines that may include job listings.

You should join at least one such organization—often, your employer will have a policy of paying for all or part of your membership, and encourage you to be active in the group. And if you're currently not employed? All the more reason to be a member of a trade organization, so that you can stay in touch with others in your industry and keep your knowledge and skills up to date.

Employment agencies

The function of an employment agency is to match job-seekers—that's *you*—with employee-seekers. Typically when you enlist the services of an employment agency, you fill out a profile and interview with an agency representative, who then takes the information and seeks a match with a company client.

Often an agency will specialize in a particular industry or field. For example, some agencies may specialize in placing secretaries, administrative assistants, and office workers. Another may focus on medical technicians.

When considering working with an employment agency, be sure you understand what your financial commitment might be. It's more common for the employer to pay any agency fees if a job match is made. *But,* you may be required to pay the agency for its services, and the terms of payment vary from agency to agency. For example, you may be required to pay an amount equivalent to one month's salary.

When seeking a job through an employment agency, make sure you understand all the terms and conditions before you sign an agreement.

Newspaper "want ads"

You've probably read the statistics that as many as 80 percent of all job openings are never advertised. While this may be true, it certainly doesn't make sense to ignore the classified ads in your community newspaper. Sunday's edition is always fat with job listings, typically categorized by field. But keep a few things in mind as you check off possibilities to contact on Monday morning.

Blind box ads are used by companies that don't want to be identified, and they pay extra for the privilege. Respond to blind ads if the position seems right for you, but don't expect much. Often, companies will place such an ad simply to see what the pool of available talent is like. (Be wary, too, that the blind ad you read hasn't been placed by your current employer! You can usually submit a response to the box office, and ask that it not be passed on to certain firms.)

Also realize that newspaper want ads tend to draw the biggest deluge of resumes. Just like you, every other job-seeker is seeing the ad and will likely be preparing a resume to send off first thing Monday. So, your resume will be sitting in a pile of anywhere from a few dozen to hundreds.

Advertisements in trade journals and magazines related to your field may be a little more targeted. But, of course, that means the others who are responding to the ad probably have more targeted experience, as well. So your competition may be a little stiffer.

College placement offices

Of course, if you're poised to enter the "real world" soon, be sure to contact your school's placement office at least by the beginning of your last semester of school. Often, such placement offices have some good connections with desirable employers who are looking for top-notch, entry-level candidates.

However, even if you've been out of school for a number of years, it might be a good idea to contact your *alma mater.* You never know what this may lead to.

Job fairs

Just like with the Sunday want ads, you'll be competing with a larger pool of candidates at these well-attended job fairs. But it's just another opportunity to drop off resumes with many companies and save time, travel, and postage. You won't have to provide a cover letter, and—if your timing is right—you might even have a chance for an impromptu interview right on the spot!

Check the Sunday classified section for listings of upcoming job fairs. They're common in college towns as well as cities with high demand for workers. Most job fairs are free, but occasionally you may run across one that charges an admission.

Build your network!

You've noticed I used the term "network" a few times in the previous sections. What exactly is a network? It is your collection of relationships—including co-workers, colleagues, industry connections, even friends and relatives—that may connect you to your next job opportunity!

Many people think of networking as meeting strangers in social circumstances, and shoving a business card in their hand and then calling them up to ask for a job.

Networking, however, should *never* be a forceful or forced action, but rather the slow building of relationships. As you build these relationships, you'll of course share information about yourself, help your contacts when you can, and turn to them for advice and help when you need it.

While it's true that, one day, you may turn to one of your networking contacts from a trade association and ask if he or she knows of a job opening that might match your experience, it's just as likely that you'll offer that contact some job leads—or that your contact will introduce you to someone in the industry who provides you with knowledge that makes you do your job better—and that leads to a promotion—which leads to interest from an outside employer.

Networks work in wondrous ways. The secret is to make your network broad and inclusive. Join business organizations, volunteer in a community effort, participate in your kids' school activities, get to know others in your company better. You never know where important connections will come from.

How to pursue that job lead

Once you've learned about a job opportunity, whether it's through a networking contact, an online job board, or a trade publication, you aren't necessarily ready to zap off your resume—yet.

Before you do anything, *research, research, research!* Whenever possible, call the company to find out exactly what they do, and the name of the person who would be your supervisor. Visit your local library to read up on the company.

This cannot be overemphasized, because applicants who show knowledge of a company stand a much better chance of being hired—or at least interviewed—by that company.

Don't forget that there may be hundreds of others applying for the same position you are. You want to do everything in your power to set yourself apart from the others.

Learn everything you can about the company, the position, and your supervisor. That way you can customize your resume, your cover letter, and even your responses in the interview to closely match the interests and needs of your prospective employer.

The cover letter

Create a custom cover letter using key facts about the company's market, product lines, and current condition. Even if you only change the first two lines of your cover letter, this helps differentiate you from the pack of applicants who seem to send resumes to every company on earth. Of course, research isn't possible with blind ads, but you can still write a letter emphasizing keywords used in the job posting.

The one thing your cover letter should *not* do is repeat the details that are found in your resume. You can certainly elaborate on some point made in your resume, but you don't want to waste space reiterating what already appears there.

The cover letter is also a good place to clarify situations that might be confusing to the reader. Let's say your resume indicates years of experience as a day-care worker, and you are pursuing a job as a crafts shop workshop leader. You might use your cover letter to point out that your favorite aspect of your current job is leading and planning the craft projects for your preschool charges.

How long should a cover letter be? Never more than one page. You want to lead with a catchy introduction that focuses on the needs of the employer—not your needs. Then you want to identify three or four points that are additional to the resume. And finally you want to conclude with some action plan—such as, "I'll follow up next week to see if you have any questions or would like to schedule an interview."

Chapter 11

At Last: The Interview

Congratulations—your standout resume is starting to generate job interviews! As I've said before, a resume won't get you a job; it's merely a door-opener. But now, your interview is your chance to elaborate on the skills and experience you've showcased so successfully in your resume—and to make a personal connection with the individual you hope to work with in the near future. It's your opportunity to go for the close, as they say in the world of sales. So it's absolutely essential that you go into the interview process with the information and skills you need to *make* that close.

Books have been written on the topic of interviewing, but in this chapter, I'll offer some of the key tips and secrets for conducting a job-winning interview:

Research the company and position

I stressed in the previous chapter the importance of learning as much as possible about the job opportunities you are pursuing *before* developing your resume and cover letter, and sending them off. I emphasize again, even more strongly, how important it is to walk into the company with a clear understanding of the corporate culture and, specifically, the job environment *you'll* be working in.

Not only do you want to know facts such as the size of the company, locations, chief activities, annual revenues, and plans for the future—you'll want to know about the *culture* of the company, as well. Why? If, for example, you walk into the interview knowing that this is a very traditional company, you'll present yourself as more conservative, perhaps focusing on your steadfastness and reliability, your long tenure at previous jobs. You may dress in the traditional "interview" attire—a dark suit. You'll probably avoid talking about the value of radical change and how you pushed for cutting-edge management changes in your previous job.

Researching the prospective employer will also help you formulate some good questions for your interviewer.

Practice your answers

While it's true that you can't predict exactly what you'll be asked in the interview, you'll have some idea of the types of questions to prepare for. "Tell me about yourself." "What is it you like best about the work you do?" "What are your weaknesses?"

At the very least, you should prepare a response to the question, "Tell me about yourself." Often, what interviewers are assessing with this question is your ability to communicate what's *important.* If you go off on a tangent about where you were born and what your hobbies are, you're not really focusing on your interviewer's interests. Prepare a brief little speech—no more than a couple minutes long—that sums up your work experience and relates it to the needs of the person you're talking to.

If you feel you need help in preparing for other commonly asked interview questions, check the Appendix at the end of this book for some great books on the topic.

Present a professional image

Often, the dark-suit model of professional dress does not apply to situations in which work is physical or, as they say, "blue collar." So, why, then, wear a "white collar" to an interview for such a job?

First of all, this is another case in which your research of the company and job will come in handy. What is the corporate "climate"? Is it ultra-casual? Even though you may be applying for a job as a laborer, you may have to interview with management or office types.

It may be true that in some cases, dressing more casually for an interview for a blue collar job will be entirely appropriate. After all, you may be seeking a job in which you'll wear a uniform. But if you dress "up" for the interview, it's unlikely that this will work against you. And it just make work *for* you. As a rule, it's always safe to wear a suit—whether for women or men—to an interview, no matter what the job is.

Whatever you choose to wear, make sure that your appearance is flawless—your clothes are clean and unwrinkled.

Arrive on time!

Your punctuality is an important measure to a prospective employer of your reliability. Do whatever you have to in order to arrive at the interview on time. In fact, work to get there about 10 minutes early. This'll give you time to collect yourself, review your notes and resume, and enter into the meeting with a calm and positive attitude.

Job Search Facts

Speak up! An Accountemps/Robert Half survey polled 150 executives from the nation's 1,000 largest companies. Can you believe that a third said that during interviews, applicants are often *too humble* in recounting their own achievements? The lesson: Don't take anything for granted, or assume employers already know how great you are. When you're called in for an interview, don't overwhelm the listener and brag about yourself, but by the same token, don't downplay your abilities.

Be positive

No matter what—you were given horrible directions, the office was hard to find, traffic was terrible—start off your interview with a positive attitude. Your interviewer wants to talk to someone who conveys enthusiasm, optimism, and eagerness. No matter what sort of day you've had, keep a smile on your face and think positive!

Don't be nervous.

An interview is not a life-or-death situation. Relax and just be yourself. Remember that you're not the only person who will be interviewed for the job. The employer may be interviewing other candidates who come across more relaxed and confident, but don't have the skills and experience you have. Don't let them get your job!

The interview is another chance to discover and market your potential, while learning more about what the employer really wants. Keep in mind that *you're* there to interview the company, as well. You shouldn't feel as if the burden is all on *your* shoulders to make a good impression.

Any decent interviewer understands that you may be nervous, especially if it's one of your very first interviews. He or she should know how to put you at ease right from the start with some light conversation, rather than put you on the spot—but don't count on it.

Some interviewers actually enjoy intimidating candidates with out-of-this-world questions or impossible situations to see how you react under pressure. Just keep in mind that it's all a show to see what you're made of. Retain your composure as much as possible, thoughtfully consider your replies, and maintain eye contact with the interviewer when responding.

Job Search Tip

When's the best time to book an interview? Believe it or not, it can make a difference. An AccounTemps survey, published in *The Chicago Tribune,* polled 200 executives. It found that job applicants who interview in the morning may be viewed more favorably than those with interviews later in the day.

Fully 83 percent of those responding said they preferred to interview candidates between *9 a.m. and 11 a.m!* No other time of day even came close. In general, hiring managers said they dislike interviewing near their usual break times.

Keep your personal life out of the interview

You may be aware that your interviewer is prohibited by law from asking certain questions about your personal life. Questions that attempt to ascertain your ethnic background, marital status, sexual activity, physical or mental health are off-limits.

There's a reason for this. So, in the course of the interview, be careful not to *offer* personal information. The interview is not the place to talk about how excited you are about your upcoming wedding, or how you're eager to supplement your family income so you can start a family.

Of course you're not perfect, and that's really not what employers expect. Sometimes, they just want to hire someone who seems to have the right kind of skills, the right type of background, and who they think they can train in their way of doing things.

I can guarantee that employers are more interested in hiring someone who seems reliable, trainable, and a "good fit" with their company culture. A company can always train you in a specific task or procedure, but they can't change your personality and make you "fit in" to their work environment.

That's why, above all, the interview is a chance to show your interviewer that you do indeed "fit" with the personality of the company as well as those you'll work with.

Chapter 12 ———————————

Resume
Samples
And More

TERRY A. LAFF
2645 Marlin Avenue
Schaumburg, IL 60193
847/555-0596

Clyde Franklin
March 5, 1999
Northwest Airlines
Minneapolis-St. Paul International Airport
St. Paul, MN 55111

Dear Mr. Franklin:

I am seeking a position as Aircraft Dispatcher with your company, and have enclosed my resume for your review. Specifically, I would like to better utilize my experience in aircraft dispatching, flight and ground instruction, and ground operations with a major commercial airline company such as Northwest Airlines.

* As Aircraft Dispatcher/Crew Scheduler at UFS, Inc., d/b/a United Express, I am in charge of daily dispatch operations coordinating ATP commuter flights and, on a rotational basis, scheduling crews.

* In addition, I am currently a part-time instructor at the Aircraft Flight Dispatcher Training Center.

Prior to UFS, I worked as an intern at American Flyers. There, I gained a solid foundation in ground operations and flight/ground instruction, after having earned an Associate of Science degree in business aviation.

I am available for an interview at your convenience. Please contact me soon to arrange a meeting. I look forward to your response.

Thank you for your time and consideration.

Sincerely,

Terry A. Laff

Enclosure

JOSEPH SLAVICEK
406 South State Street
Elgin, IL 60123
847/555-8017

Mr. Tony Boxit
Total Shippers, Inc.
2345 N. Locust Steet
Itasca, IL 60148

Dear Mr. Boxit:

I am pursuing opportunities with Total Shippers, Inc. in Distribution or Warehouse Operations. My background is in Distribution Management, with extensive experience at both line and staff-level supervision in union and non-union environments.

For the past 10 years, I have been deeply involved in RF materials management systems. I've directed all aspects of RF from implementation to training and enhancements to second generation upgrades. Primarily, though, I bring demonstrated ability to provide ongoing training and development as well as a commitment to and pride in the results of my efforts.

I am available for an interview at your earliest convenience, and can provide solid references at your request. Please let me know when we may meet. I look forward to your response, and thank you for your time and consideration.

Sincerely,

Joseph Slavicek

Enc.

THOMAS G. MINO
661 Pinewood Lane
Bloomingale, IL 60108
708/555-3052

August 22, 1999

Samuel Haber
K.L. Smith Company
724 Eden Way
Elgin, IL 60120

Dear Mr. Haber:

I am exploring employment opportunities with your company and have enclosed my resume for your review. Specifically, I would like to better utilize my experience in transportation as a driver/courier.

Throughout my career, I've proven my ability to work effectively with management and staff at all levels of experience. Most importantly, I have demonstrated my ability to provide exceptional transportation service in a fast-paced environment and to handle significant volume-related pressure.

* My background includes full responsibility for the timely and accurate delivery of confidential and sensitive materials.

* I am self-motivated and energetic, and communicate well with people.

* Being detail-oriented, I take it upon myself to check all aspects of the delivery instructions I receive and to make corrections when necessary.

I can provide excellent references, and am available for an interview at your convenience to discuss how my experience can benefit your company. Please contact me at the above number in order to arrange a meeting. I look forward to meeting you.

Thank you for your time and consideration.

Sincerely,

Thomas G. Mino

Enclosure

THOMAS P. MUNICH
118 North Rockwell
Chicago, IL 60659
312/555-5179

September 13, 1999

Sylvia Rothman
Oasis Heating and Cooling, Inc.
7127 Sherwood Drive
Forest Park, IL 60130

Dear Ms. Rothman:

Given the expanding housing market in the Chicago metropolitan area, the demand for quality HVAC installations and repair has never been greater. I recently received Certification in HVAC systems, and am certain my education in state-of-the-art equipment can benefit your customers and your company.

My previous experience and training from the Environmental Technical Institute has given me expertise in:

- The teardown and troubleshooting of air conditioners, gas and electric furnaces, and a wide range of equipment including humidifiers.

- Effectively working with customers to determine and meet their needs in a friendly yet business-like manner.

Throughout my employment I've proven my ability to work well with people and provide quick, professional service. I am very self-motivated, with an excellent record of customer satisfaction.

I am enclosing my resume for your review. I would like to meet for an interview to discuss how my skills will benefit your company. I may be reached at the above number, and look forward to hearing from you.

Thank you for your time and consideration.

Sincerely,

Thomas P. Munich

Enclosure

JENNIFER A. BAILOUT

REFERENCES

Curt Nefort
Sales Manager / Vice President
Waterfield Financial
11115 Kenwood Road
Cincinnati, OH 45242
513/555-5400

Mindy Semiloff
Ford Consumer Finance
4034 Woodthrush Drive
Grosbeck, OH 45251
513/555-4784

John Donovan
908 Meadowland Drive
Cincinnati, OH 45255
513/555-7022

JOSEPH SLAVICEK
406 South State Street
Elgin, IL 60123
847/555-8017

Salary History

(Annual basis)

Vallen Safety Supply Company, **Warehouse Supervisor,** $43,500

Preferred Meal Systems, **Warehouse Manager,** $44,000

Panasonic, **Assistant Manager,** $38,000

Quality Distribution, **Warehouse Manager,** $35,000

Wayco Foods Corporation, **Night Superintendent,** $30,000

Superior Coffee, **Warehouse Superintendent/Production Manager,** $28,000

HEWITT C. STREAMLINE

33188 West Schick
Bloomingdale, IL 60108   hewfixit@aol.com   708/555-8047

AIRCRAFT MECHANIC

PROFILE:

- ▶ Licensed Airframe and Powerplant Mechanic; with hands-on training in structural repair and composites.
- ▶ Experience in A&P inspections, including the repair and maintenance of systems for the DC-10, DC-9, 747 and 727. Simulators include the 707 cockpit procedural trainer and 747 and L1011 maintenance videos.
- ▶ Performed repairs on the Cessna 150, 152, 172, 172RG, and various Beechcraft and Piper models.
- ▶ Conversant in Spanish; familiar with Windows and MS Works.
- ▶ Skilled in the use of lathes and standard shop equipment, as well as:
  - → Fiberglass and bonded honeycomb repair
  - → Weighing and balancing of control surfaces
  - → Removal and replacement of skin panels and aircraft fasteners
  - → Manufacture and testing of control cables
  - → Comprehensive modification of aircraft structures
  - → Corrosion control and aircraft painting

EDUCATION:

Southern Illinois University, Carbondale, IL
B.S. Degree: Aviation Management   Graduated 5/92
A.A.S. Degree: Aviation Maintenance Technologies   Graduated 12/90
→ Alpha Eta Rho, Professional Aviation Fraternity

EMPLOYMENT:

Tapco Corporation (ASLS / Manpower), Wood Dale, IL   9/92-Present
Warehouseman
Responsible for data entry/retrieval on a Windows database, as well as production scheduling.
Duties include the shearing of copper-clad laminate for printed circuit boards.
Occasionally supervise up to six employees in stocking, inventory control and forklift operation for truck loading and unloading.

Heating / Air Conditioning Service   Part-time, 9/92-Present
Install and maintain furnaces and air conditioners at residential properties.

Tim's VW Restoration, Carbond.ale, IL   1987-1992
Technician / Assistant Manager
Performed engine/body rebuilding and inventory control.

Valley Heating and Air Conditioning, Hinsdale, IL   Summers, 1988-1989
Repairman

JAMES R. MOXIE

34254 Tomahawk Court
Carol Stream, IL 60188   708/555-2770

AIRCRAFT MECHANIC

PROFILE:

▶ Licensed as: Airframe Mechanic, Powerplant Mechanic, Commercial Pilot, single and multi-engine instrument, Certified Flight Instructor, single engine and instrument, Instrument Ground Instructor and Advanced Ground Instructor.

▶ Skilled in a variety of shop procedures and equipment including:

→ Fiberglass and bonded honeycomb repair
→ Balancing of control surfaces
→ Removal and replacement of skin panels and aircraft fasteners
→ Manufacture of control cables
→ Comprehensive modification of aircraft structures
→ Corrosion control and aircraft painting
→ Sheet metal repair

EMPLOYMENT:

United Express, Chicago, IL   1/95-Present
Aircraft Mechanic
Responsible for the maintenance and repair of a Part 121 Airline large turboprop aircraft (ATP).

Industrial Air Charter, Naperville, IL   3/90-1/95
Aircraft Mechanic
Scheduled inspections and provided regular maintenance of single and light twin-engine aircraft for a Part 135 Cargo Operator.
Compiled and updated aircraft maintenance log books.

Eldon Office Products, Itasca, IL
Assistant Manager   1/86-4/89
Supervised 10 employees in various warehouse activities including order picking, packing and loading/unloading merchandise.
Inspected inbound shipments for discrepancies, and effectively coordinated the resolution of problems with branch managers and customers.
Performed the duties of Warehouse Manager as required.

Shipper   10/83-1/86
Packed outbound merchandise according to customer orders.
Scheduled and monitored shipments working with various truck lines; resolved problems promptly.
Completed and distributed shipping documents.

EDUCATION:

College of DuPage, Glen Ellyn, IL   1986-1988
Completed courses in general studies.

Glenbard North High School, Carol Stream, IL   Graduated 1984

TERRY B. SAFE

2645 Marlin Avenue
Schaumburg, IL 60193   847/555-0596

OBJECTIVE: *AIRCRAFT DISPATCHER*
Aircraft Dispatcher Certified, March 1996.

PROFILE:
- ▶ Coordinate crew/flight routings and prepare dispatch releases, utilizing the Apollo system and Kavouras weather tracking system, in compliance with FARs and company policies/procedures; skilled in decision-making and problem-solving; effectively handle multiple priorities.
- ▶ *Additional Certifications*:

Flight Instructor-Instrument	December 1994
Flight Instructor-Airplane	December 1994
Commercial Pilot	November 1994
Advanced Instrument Ground Instructor	June 1994
Instrument Rating	February 1994
Private Pilot	June 1989

EMPLOYMENT: UFS, Inc., d/b/a United Express, Chicago, IL   1996-Present
Aircraft Dispatcher / Crew Scheduler
In charge of daily dispatch operations for nine UFS-owned ATP 64-seat aircraft, including weather checks, routing, crew/aircraft selection and fuel loads, for this commuter airline.
Generate dispatch releases and secure final signoffs from assigned Captains.
- → Maintain crew schedules for 180 crew members.

The Hertz Corporation, Chicago, IL   1995-1996
City Revenue Manager
Hired, trained, scheduled and managed 80 counter representatives and 50 shuttle bus drivers in providing rental car services, with responsibility for daily sales.

American Flyers, West Chicago, IL   1993-1995
Internship / Operations Manager and Flight / Ground Instructor
Scheduled flight students, instructors and aircraft for daily flight training lessons.
Administered flight/ground instruction operations within budget guidelines.
- → Conducted private, instrument, commercial and CFI/CFII ground schools.

Prior Employment
Assistant Store Manager, T.J. Maxx   1990-1993
Area Sales Manager, Sears Roebuck and Company   1986-1990

EDUCATION: Airline Flight Dispatcher Training Center, Inc., Elk Grove, IL   1996
Certificate: Aircraft Dispatcher
Employed as a part-time instructor, 1996-Present

Inver Hills Community College, Inver Grove Heights, MN   1993
Associate of Science degree in business aviation

HAROLD RINGER

1776 Norwood #G-8
Itasca, IL 60143
708/555-7933

ALARM TECHNICIAN

EXPERIENCE:
- Skilled in the installation and wiring of residential and commercial alarms, control panels and keypads by Digital Control Systems, as well as a full range of motion detectors.

- Experience with virtually all types of accessories; skills applicable to new products and business environments.

- Current License, Department of Professional Regulation, expires 9/1/06.

EMPLOYMENT: <u>Emergency Networks, Inc.,</u> Alarm Company, Itasca, IL   3/97–Present
Lead Technician
Responsible for prompt, effective installations of residential and commercial alarm systems listed above.

<u>Lock-Up Storage,</u> Evanston, IL   6/94–8/94
Elevator Operator

MILITARY: <u>U.S. Army,</u> Fort Drum, NY   10/94–7/96
Infantry
* Honorable Discharge
* Army Service Ribbon
* Rifle Expert Badge
* Completed basic training at AIT, Fort Benning, GA. Served 13 Weeks.

EDUCATION: <u>Professional Truck Driving School,</u> Chicago, IL   8/96–11/96
CDL License

<u>Sparta High School,</u> Sparta, WI
Graduate   1994

JOHN B. URBAN

702 Kool Avenue
Streamwood, IL 60107 708/555-0412

OBJECTIVE: *ASSEMBLY / DISTRIBUTION*
A position where skills in inventory control, tracking, and hydraulic valve assembly would be of value.

PROFILE:
- ► More than three years in the assembly of hydraulic valves from as few as three parts to as many as 20.
- ► Experience in the setup and organization of warehousing and distribution operations; utilize Fourth Shift data entry software.
- ► Staff training and supervision in warehousing and distribution procedures.
- ► Fluent in Polish.

EMPLOYMENT: Sterling Hydraulics, Inc., Schaumburg, IL 8/91-present
Shipping and Receiving Clerk
Responsible for the accurate inventory, shipping and receiving of hydraulic valve parts for this $7 million company.
Compile and maintain all records of receivables on a daily basis.
Trained and supervised a crew in shipping/receiving and distribution operations.
Assemble various hydraulic valves.
- → Set up procedures for arranging stock room at the end of the shift.
- → Arrange orderly setup of valve parts.
- → Prepare all paperwork for shipping via UPS and Federal Express.
- → Operate forklift for truck loading/unloading, stocking, picking and cycle counting.
- → Utilize automated computer system for data entry regarding inventory tracking for receivables.

Amp, Inc., Schaumburg, IL 1988-7/91
Shipping and Receiving Clerk
Handled prompt receiving, shipping, order picking/packing and storage of supplies.
Operated forklift for loading/unloading trailers on a busy dock.

First Impressions, Elk Grove Village, IL 1987-1988
Shipping and Receiving Clerk
Performed general warehouse duties including receiving and picking/packing orders.

Polyline, Des Plaines, IL 1985-1987
Shipping and Receiving Clerk
Various warehouse and distribution responsibilities.

Ludwig Industries, Chicago, IL 1976-1985
Receiving Clerk
General warehouse receiving/shipping, picking/packing and distribution duties.

EDUCATION: Harold Washington College, Chicago, IL
Completed one year of courses in Law Enforcement 1975-1976
Prosser Vocational High School, Chicago, IL Graduated 1975

ZACK BEACH

67812 Castlewood Lane
Bartlett, IL 60109   708/555-9649

ASSEMBLY / PRODUCTION

PROFILE:
▶ Extensive background in the assembly and installation of electrical components and machine parts, on job sites and production lines.

▶ Skilled in troubleshooting and promptly taking corrective action; read and interpret blueprints/bills of materials; adhere to safety policies, procedures and codes.

▶ Utilize ARC and MIG welders, micrometers, air gun nailers, torque wrenches, hammers, screwdrivers, drill presses, shears, Whitney press; operate forklifts and cranes.

EMPLOYMENT:
Beardsley and Piper, Inc., Chicago, IL   1/94–Present
Assembler
Primarily assemble foundry machines and roofing lines for clients in diverse regions including China and Vietnam; adhere to blueprint and bill of materials specifications.

Coiltech, Schiller Park, IL   10/92-12/93
Service Representative
Installed, connected, tested and adjusted new electrical equipment including coils, stackers and slitting lines, for large-scale machinery. Utilized rod and MIG welders extensively.
→ Traveled to customer sites in Midwest and West.

Beardsley and Piper, Inc., Chicago, IL   1/87-9/92
Assembler
Operated a crane and standard pallet forklifts to assemble and install such parts as large overhead frames.
Performed shipping/receiving activities including packing crate boxes for domestic and international orders.

Littel, Inc., Chicago, IL   4/85-12/86
Assembler
Operated automated equipment to assemble and inspect a variety of products including pop cans and automobile hoods, doors and fenders.

Lucas Tire, Chicago, IL   10/84-4/85
Automobile Mechanic
Repaired and maintained a variety of automobiles for individual customers, servicing an average of 15 cars per month.

EDUCATION:
Lincoln Technical Institute, Norridge, IL   Graduated 1984
Diploma: Automotive and Diesel Mechanic

Weber High School, Chicago, IL   Graduated 1983

SUSAN B. SASSY

23180 S. Waters Edge Drive #102
Glendale Heights, IL 60139   630/555-1402

AUDIO / VISUAL PRODUCTION

PROFILE:
- Skilled in all aspects of sound production and technical direction for radio, special events and the theater, including recording, dubbing, editing and final mix-down.
- Radio Disc Jockey experience includes voice overs, commercials, public service announcements (PSAs) and news writing/reporting.
- Background in the setup of 8- and 12-channel soundboards, amplifiers, microphones, loudspeakers and related equipment.
- Familiar with Windows 95, MS Word and WordPerfect.

PRODUCTION EXPERIENCE:

Village Theatre Guild, Glen Ellyn, IL   1991-present
Technical Director: Sound *and* Member (Volunteer)
In charge of all sound setups for numerous theatrical productions.
Function as Stage Manager and oversee lighting, sound design and set decoration.
→ Chairman: House Supplies, 1994–1995
→ Chairman: Membership, 1992–1993
→ Chairman: Vending Concessions, 1994–present.
   Realized a 1000% profit

Audio Visual Techniques, Elk Grove Village, IL   1982-1983
Audio Visual Technician: Set up and maintained A.V. equipment for meetings and special events at Oak Brook and O'Hare Marriott locations.

Sheraton-Naperville Hotel, Naperville, IL   1981-1982
Convention Setup: Assembled stages, chairs, tables and audio/visual equipment.

OTHER EMPLOYMENT:

Good Samaritan Hospital, Downers Grove, IL   1983-Present
Senior Supply Services Clerk
Responsible for a staff of 10 and a medical product inventory of $500,000.
Act as training instructor (preceptor) for new employees.
→ Twice awarded the Good Samaritan "That's the Spirit" award.

Disk Jockey / Announcer experience at:
WKKD AM/FM, Aurora, IL, Adult Contemporary Music   3/87-12/87
WRAJ AM/FM, Anna, IL, Adult Contemporary   1980-1981

EDUCATION:

Southern Illinois University, Carbondale, IL   1979-1981
B.S. Degree, Studied Radio-Television Broadcasting and Speech Communications

PERSONAL:

Water's Edge Condominium Association, Glendale Hts., IL   7/95-Present
President and Board of Directors

RICHARD L. SMASH

2358 Aberdeen Court
Schaumburg, IL 60194   847/555-7056

AUTO COLLISION REPAIR MANAGEMENT

PROFILE:
- ▸ Extensive background in virtually all aspects of automotive collision repair operations management, including production, sales and office functions, in compliance with industry standards and practices.

- ▸ Skilled in salesmanship, troubleshooting, billing/job cost estimating, materials/parts procurement and inventory control; well-versed in preferred insurance practices.

- ▸ Hire, train and supervise technicians in mechanical craftsmanship, technical applications, quality control and flagship customer service.

- ▸ Utilize Mitchell, ADP and CCC estimating systems; ASE certified in body paint, steering/suspension and AC, and in AC recovery and repair; efficiently operate Chief frame machines, the electronic Chief Genesis measuring system and the FMC four-wheel alignment system.

EMPLOYMENT: Wally's CarStar, Des Plaines, IL   1979-Present
A collision repair franchise with $1.25 million in average annual revenues.
Production Manager   1/84-Present
Supervise up to seven body and paint technicians in daily job assignments, with attention to detail to meet delivery deadlines and quality standards.
Provide on-the-job training, schedule and assign jobs, and evaluate worker performance.
Handle customer inquiries and troubleshooting; communicate with technicians and insurance companies to resolve problems with speed and accuracy.
Order parts/supplies and monitor inventory levels.
Write up estimates for customers; work closely with State Farm and American Family insurance staff to process claims.
Process all daily cash, including cash reconciliations and bank deposit preparation.
- → Track and document information on used parts in accordance with Illinois Secretary of State regulations.
- → Rated #1 in office operations in 1994 for CarStar nationwide.

Body / Metal Technician   9/79-1/84
Replaced, repaired and refinished bodies on a wide range of U.S. and foreign vehicles, utilizing Chief and FMC equipment.

Spradlin Chevrolet, Park Ridge, IL   2/73-9/79
Collision Repair Technician
Gained valuable experience in automotive repair activities.

EDUCATION: Denver Diesel and Automotive College, Denver, CO   9/72-1/73
Certificate: Basic Collision Course

Maine East High School, Park Ridge, IL

95

VICTOR A. WHEEL

3241 Thorn
Keeneyville, IL 60172   708/555-0954

OBJECTIVE: **AUTOMOTIVE MECHANIC**
A position where hands-on skills would be utilized.

EXPERIENCE:
- Skilled in the repair and maintenance of auto and truck gas and diesel engines and transmissions.
- Handle diagnostic testing on computerized systems; experience in complete teardowns and rebuilds.
- Repair and maintain light and medium duty trucks, autos, mowers, pumps and tractors.
- Trained in auto mechanics at Southern Illinois Vocational/Technical Institute.

EMPLOYMENT: Krimson Valley Landscape Co., Roselle, IL   1989-Present
Mechanic
Responsible for repair and ongoing maintenance for up to 25 trucks and automobiles, as well as landscape equipment such as mowers and tractors. Organize job and maintenance schedules.
Previously supervised up to 10 employees in professional landscaping operations.
* Work effectively with staff, management and customers as required.

4B RV - Recreational Vehicles, Streamwood, IL   1988-1989
Mechanic
Repaired all types of RV motors and drivetrains, as well as internal systems for plumbing and HVAC.
Performed all mechanic's duties for used cars and campers.

Sports and Classic Restorations, Itasca, IL   1987-1988
Mechanic
Worked primarily with classic and sports cars.

Long Chevrolet, Elmhurst, IL   1984-1987
Line Mechanic
Responsible for all types of repair on new and used automobiles.

Ray's Arco, Bensenville, IL   1982-1984
Mechanic
Worked on all makes and models of small trucks and cars.

EDUCATION: Southern Illinois University, Carbondale, IL   1982
Earned Certificate in Auto Mechanics

Driscoll High School, Addison, IL   Graduated 1980

DON BOOKMAN

22616 Plamondon
Addison, IL 60101

630/555-2660

BINDERY OPERATIONS

PROFILE:

▶ Extensive background in virtually all aspects of finishing operations for printed materials, including sales, production and office supervision responsibilities in team environments.

▶ Train and supervise employees in cutting, folding and stitching activities, as well as daily equipment/tool maintenance and repair; maintain quality standards and compliance with customer specifications.

▶ Operate machinery including Lawson, Siebold and Polar paper cutters; Muller Martini, McCainn, Omega and Consolidated stitchers; Baum and MBO folders; 3-knife book trimmers; and RB-5 Perfect binders.

EMPLOYMENT:

Kelvyn Press, Broadview, IL   10/92-Present
Finishing Supervisor
Organize, coordinate and schedule 12 employees in finishing activities for a wide range of commercial jobs, for this printer with sales revenues of $12-$15 million.
Provide on-the-job training; evaluate and document individual performance.
Work closely with Sales to assess and meet customer specifications.
Procure, setup and maintain equipment in accordance with job requirements.

→ Requested by Muller Martini to demonstrate its saddle-stitching machinery to a prospective client.

Olympic Bindery, Broadview, IL   1/85-10/92
President / Co-Owner
Responsible for the setup and operation of this binding company, as a member of a two-partner team, with responsibility for sales, administration and production.
Hired, trained and managed up to 32 employees in cutting, folding and stitching.

→ Negotiated the lease for a 18,000 sq. ft. facility; configured the layout and purchased/installed the equipment.

→ Handled a variety of jobs such as AMOCO credit card applications, PERT crack 'n peel stickers and Ed McMahon/Clearinghouse sweepstake materials.

→ Key clients included Soodik Printing, Berlin Industries and J.J. Collins.

→ Achieved $1 million in sales and developed a client base of 100 accounts.

Progressive Bindery, Clyo, IL   4/81-12/84
Foreman
Supervised up to 30 employees in production activities.

Bell Litho, Elk Grove Village, IL   3/79-4/81
Combination Operator

Photo Press, Broadview, IL   1/74-3/79
Finishing Technician
Gained initial experience in cutting, folding and stitching jobs.

EDUCATION:

Rezinorr High School, Chicago, IL

JAMES A. HOUSEMAN

2357 North Sheridan Road, #3B
Chicago, IL 60660   708/555-0257 or 312/555-2004

OBJECTIVE: **Building Maintenance**
A position where maintenance and mechanical expertise would be utilized in a team environment.

EXPERIENCE:
- ▸ Proven ability to maintain buildings and mechanical equipment, including contracting outside services, troubleshooting and handling tenant requests professionally.

- ▸ EPA Certified for Type I maintenance; expert in HVAC systems: refrigeration, air conditioning, heating and electronics.

- ▸ Skilled in various trades and maintenance, repair and installation services:

→ Plumbing	→ Electrical
→ HVAC	→ Carpentry
→ Drywall	→ Tile
→ Pest Control	→ Floor

EMPLOYMENT: Village Park, Westmont, IL   1994–Present
Building Maintenance Supervisor
Responsible for maintaining plumbing, electrical systems, boilers, lighting, and other repair and mechanical work of this 400-unit apartment complex.

233 East Walton, Chicago, IL   1989–1993
Building Engineer
In charge of maintaining common areas of this first-class condominium building, including heating, ventilation and other utilities; assisted tenants in repairs and maintenance.

El Lago Condominium Association, Chicago, IL   1987–1988
Building Maintenance Technician
Responsible for general maintenance of boilers, circulating pumps and cooling towers.

Park Sheridan Apartments, Chicago, IL   1985–1987
Assistant Building Engineer

Malibu East Condominium Association, Chicago, IL   1982–1985
Building Maintenance Technician

CERTIFICATION: EPA Certification, Type I   1993
Air Conditioning Contractors of America

**ADVANCED
TRAINING:**   HVAC Systems, Janitors Local #1   1985

THOMAS MEATMAN

2204 Oak St.
Roselle, IL 60172

708/555-1858

OBJECTIVE: ***BUTCHER / MANAGER***
A position utilizing extensive meat and food merchandising expertise.

EXPERIENCE:
- Proven abilities in all aspects of butchering, retail meat processing and merchandising, including quality control and staff management.

- Train and motivate meat processing personnel; conduct training sessions on meat products; consult and communicate with senior retail managers and store owners on merchandising.

- Develop and implement cost-effective inventory control procedures and policies; plan and prepare product displays.

EMPLOYMENT: <u>Dominick's Stores and predecessors (National Tea, A & P and Wieboldt's)</u>
Various positions

<u>Buffalo Grove, IL store</u>
Meat Cutter   6/93-Present
Responsible for solving meat department operational problems; handle meat product processing; train department personnel.

<u>Two Hoffman Estates, IL stores</u>
Meat Department Manager   1966-1993
Directed and supervised entire meat department operation, including processing and quality control; set up product displays, trained and supervised up to 10 employees.

<u>Several Chicago-area suburban stores</u>
Meat Processing Training Specialist   1964-1966
Planned and conducted training sessions in meat product management and merchandising for meat department managers and line personnel.

EDUCATION: <u>J.B. Conant High School</u>, Hoffman Estates, IL   Graduated 1964

HAMMER T. NAIL

2811 Amelia
Addison, IL 60101   708/555-9335

OBJECTIVE: *CARPENTRY / CONSTRUCTION*
A position where proven skills would be of value.

EXPERIENCE:
- Skilled in Carpentry, Woodworking and Cabinetry, including project supervision from excavation to trim.
- Train and supervise work crews in commercial/residential remodeling and new construction projects; coordinate schedules and all trades.
- Handle material and supply ordering, as well as vendor/customer relations and quality control.

EMPLOYMENT: <u>J.S. Adams, Inc.</u>, Des Plaines, IL   1984–Present
Journeyman Carpenter
Responsible for all types of carpentry, including framing and final trim work for commercial and residential remodeling and new construction projects throughout the Chicagoland area.
Supervise up to 50 carpenters and other professionals in electrical work, plumbing, brick laying, roofing, HVAC, concrete forming and excavating.
Order materials and blueprint updates; consistently meet strict time constraints.
Experience with hundreds of projects including:
* Addition: A major nursing home.
* Remodeling: Emergency Room, Michael Reese Hospital.
* Addition/Remodeling: A major food processing plant.
* Remodeling: A major youth academy.
* Addition: A 30–door loading dock for a major bread company.

<u>Mayfair Construction</u>, Chicago, IL   1983-1984
Commercial Carpenter

<u>Tureck Construction</u>, Chicago, IL   1976-1983
Residential Carpenter and Trim Foreman
Supervised a wide range of carpentry and trim work for custom-built homes in Lincolnshire, IL.
Supervised up to 20 employees in all procedures.

<u>Corona Furniture</u>, Chicago, IL   1968-1976
Custom Furniture Maker
Responsible for complete fabrication of custom, ornate furniture, including replicas of desks and cabinets.
Operated and maintained all tools in a complete mill shop.

PERSONAL: Self-motivated and professional.
Willing to begin at entry-level and advance with a well run company.

WATTS T. DEAL

1249 Grant Circle, Apt F   Res: 708/555-0835
Streamwood, IL 60107   Cellular phone: 815/555-4969

CASINO OPERATIONS / HOSPITALITY SERVICES

PROFILE:

▶ Extensive background in customer-oriented service operations and business development, including sales, marketing, promotions and cost control.

▶ Excellent communication skills; maintain positive relations with staff and customers in high-volume, fast-paced operations.

▶ Proven ability to handle currency and financial transactions accurately; resolve discrepancies promptly; licensed by the Illinois Gaming Board.

▶ Familiar with WordPerfect 5.0, 5.1, Quattro Pro and E-mail, and the specialized systems MUTUALINK and KRONOS; utilize TRW system to run credit checks.

EMPLOYMENT: Grand Victoria, Elgin, IL   9/94–Present
Cage Supervisor
Responsible for up to 100 employees including 74 cashiers, four soft count supervisors and 13 soft count clerks in cashiering for this riverboat casino.
Monitor the KRONOS payroll reports for payroll information.
Utilize Quattro Pro to schedule cashiers and track cash over/short counts.
Run customer credit requests through the TRW credit report system.
Monitor transactions for zero-tolerance adherence to the Illinois Gaming Board regulations.
Prepare currency transaction reports (CTR) as required under Chapter 31.
Submit incident and credit fraud reports to Security personnel.
➡ Trained in the Trace Miller Company reservation booking system.
➡ Promoted from Cage/Ticketing Supervisor.

Casino Queen, East St. Louis, IL   6/93-9/94
Main Banker / Cashier
In charge of all aspects of cage/bank operations for this riverboat casino.

First State Federal Credit Union, Dover, DE   7/92-6/93
Head Teller

Army & Air Force Exchange Service, Ramstien Air Base, Germany 1990-1992
Central Checkout Supervisor   2/91-6/92

TRAINING:

▪ Frontline Leadership
▪ CUNA Star (Customer Service) Modules Training
▪ Principles of Management

Timothy A. Watcher

112 Lexington Drive #306
Mt. Prospect, IL 60056   847/555-1041

CATV LINE MAINTENANCE / SWEEP

PROFILE:

▶ Skilled in all aspects of MATV and CATV line sweep, configuration and maintenance, from head-end and nodes to fiber optic connections, cabling and indoor/outdoor installations to multiple TVs.

▶ Proficient in fine-tuning of amps and the use of taps and connectors; splice from nodes to term taps and proof prints for upgrades.

▶ Experience in staff hiring, training and supervision in all major operations, including customer communications, status reporting and quality control.

EXPERIENCE: <u>Contracts with TCI Cable Co.</u>, Mt. Prospect, IL
Contractor: ANS, Inc., Westminster, PA   4/98-9/98
Performed walkouts and proofed prints for high-quality upgrades.

Supervisor: Voltelcon, Rancho Cuca Monga, CA   2/95-3/98
Trained and supervised up to 12 in CATV upgrades, including a 750 mhz MATV upgrade for FOX Broadcasting and an upgrade for Time Warner. Utilized prints and processed node orders; routed all work and processed staff time sheets.
Produced end-of-day update prints and updated all production logs.
Worked with vendors and suppliers; ordered all materials and processed payroll.

→ Directed the MATV/CATV system setup at Fox Broadcasting in Los Angeles, including all routing, splicing and activation for numerous on-site monitors.

→ Acted as liaison with Fox executives and maintained all work schedules and quality control.

→ Lead Person with Time Warner executives for their CATV system in Oahu, HI.

Contractor: R.S. Services, Barrington, IL   9/94-2/95
Performed system upgrades including splicing and activation.
Supervised a CATV upgrade project for Continental Cable in Romeoville.

Supervisor / Service Technician: TCI, Mt. Prospect, IL   10/87-9/94
Fine-tuned amps and performed aerial construction.
Maintained systems from head-end to subscriber TV.

Prior experience with the City of Chicago installing CATV. Install and Service Technician for Lakes Cable; installed underground and aerial systems.

EDUCATION: Completed NCTI courses: Installer, Installer Tech. and Service Tech.
<u>McHenry High School</u>, McHenry, IL   **Graduate**

JOSEPH L. LADLE

5687 Woodview Drive
Medinah, IL 60157   708/555-3819

EXPERIENCE:
- Diverse experience as Chef or Sous Chef, including full responsibility for kitchen operations.
- Experience with a wide range of American, Italian and Asian cuisine, as well as French Fine Dining.
- Skilled in the complete setup and management of banquets, cafeterias and kitchens for high-volume breakfasts, luncheons and dinners.
- Effectively hire, train and supervise all levels of kitchen staff in food preparation and state-of-the-art presentation; fluent in Spanish.

EMPLOYMENT: The Point Supper Club, Bloomingdale, IL   11/94–Present
Sous Chef
Prepare a wide range of soups, appetizers and specialty dishes for this fine dining restaurant with banquet service for up to 200.
Assist in interviewing, hiring and scheduling up to 20 staff.
Handle food ordering, inventory control and kitchen supplies
* Create and prepare daily specials ranging from Asian, Seafood and Steak to Health-oriented dishes.

Indian Lakes Resort, Bloomingdale, IL   4/88-11/94
Head Chef   6/93-11/94
Responsible for 10 employees and all operations of the Frontier Grill, specializing in American Cuisine.
Supervised breakfasts, lunches and dinners for up to 700 meals per day.
Coordinated stocking, inventory control and payroll in a cost-effective manner.
* Organized all work schedules and trained/managed personnel, including a Sous Chef, Line Cooks, Pantry Chefs and Dishwashers.

Sous Chef: On-The-Pond Restaurant   7/92-6/93
Effectively hired, trained and supervised up to 20 employees in the preparation of French Fine Dining and American Cuisine.
Maintained inventories and purchased food and supply.
Handled a wide range of food service and banquet duties.
* Managed the employee restaurant, with up to 600 meals per day.

Sous Chef, Lead Line Cook and Pantry Chef
Frontier Grill   4/88-7/92

EDUCATION: Washburne Trade School, Chicago, IL
Culinary Arts Degree   4/92

Davea Vocational School, Addison, IL
Culinary Arts Program   Certificate: 6/90
Current Member: **Culinary and Pastry Arts Advisory Council**

ROSA CLERKMAN

2227 Hesterman Drive
Glendale Heights, IL 60139

708/555-7778

OBJECTIVE: A **Clerical** position where proven analytical skills and attention to detail will be utilized.

PROFILE:
- More than three years in various business environments, including office support and the research/reconciliation of reports for purchasing and inventory control.

- Perform data entry/retrieval and balance cash transactions with speed and accuracy.

- Proficient in Windows, Paradox and WordPerfect 5.1.

EMPLOYMENT: Tri Star Metals, Inc., Carol Stream, IL   4/94–Present
Office Clerk
Provide a wide range of office services in a professional manner, including data entry/retrieval of purchase orders utilizing Paradox.
Analyze and update monthly purchase order and inventory reports.
- Perform proofreading, verification and distribution of invoices.
- Conduct research to resolve discrepancies.
- Compile documentation for freight bills.

Footlocker, Bloomingdale, IL   5/92–4/94
Cashier
Responsible for customer service and sales transactions for this high volume shoe retail outlet.
Accurately handled large amounts of cash.
- Operated a computerized register system.
- Trained a new employee in professional customer service, store procedures, product lines and register operations.

Phar-Mor, Inc., Bloomingdale, IL   8/91–5/92
Cashier
Duties similar to those at Footlocker including training, customer service and computerized register transactions.

EDUCATION: College of DuPage, Glen Ellyn, IL
Associates Degree in Arts expected December, 1999

Glenbard North High School, Carol Stream, IL   1992

ALFRED A. KEYS
6614 Glen Ellyn Road #205
Bloomingdale, IL 60108
708/555-2588
alfakey@aol.com

OBJECTIVE: ***COMPUTER OPERATOR***
A position where proven technical skills would be utilized.

PROFILE:
- ▸ Familiar with DOS, Windows, Wordperfect and Prodigy.
- ▸ Knowledge of PC setup and installation, as well as various peripherals, data entry and file updating.
- ▸ Experience training individuals in system operations, as well as collections and customer service.

EMPLOYMENT: U.S. Post Office, Forest Park, IL   1994–Present
Parcel Post Distributor
Responsible for various post office functions including mail sorting.

Circuit City, Calumet City, IL   1993–1994
Computer Sales Representative
Conducted training of staff and customers in computer system setup and operations.
Gained excellent experience in system operations and various types of hardware and software.

Rent-A-Center, Riverside, CA   1990–1992
Collections / Assistant Manager
Directed and maintained collection operations related to past-due credit card accounts, including credit checks and status reporting.
Assisted in training and supervising staff in all operations.

Pro-Tel, Lansing, IL   1987–1988
Sales Representative
Handled sales of credit cards and services via telephone.

EDUCATION: Ivy Tech College, Gary, IN   1988–1990
Major: Marketing
Courses included business math, marketing, communications and human relations.

MILITARY: United States Marine Corps, Japan/Korea   1983–1987
NCO Corporal
Supervised a crew of 10, including the inventory of small arms and record keeping.
- → Earned various awards for excellent service.

MARK C. HAMMER

2266 Augusta
Elgin, IL 60120   708/555-0627

CONSTRUCTION MANAGER / SUPERINTENDENT

EXPERIENCE:
- More than 10 years in construction supervision including accurate takeoffs, estimating, budgeting, contracting, purchasing and invoicing.

- Experience in full on-site construction management and land development; effectively schedule, monitor and inspect all work from start to customer orientation.

- Work effectively with architects, engineers, developers, bankers, contractors, inspectors, city officials, decorators, agents and home buyers.

EMPLOYMENT: Pulte Home Corporation, Hoffman Estates, IL   7/87-Present
Superintendent
Responsible for contractors and all activities on site for single family and townhome projects.
Schedule, monitor and inspect all work from start to customer orientation.
* Maintain budgets, process invoices and control overhead costs.

J.H. Darnell & Sons, Dallas, TX   8/83-7/87
Joint Venture   1/85-7/87
Researched and selected subdivisions lots for custom homes valued up to $1 million.
Involved in interim finance acquisition, budgeting, contracting and interface with architects on design.
Accountable for all activities from start to customer orientation.
* Assisted in sales activities; Texas Real Estate License.

Superintendent   8/83-1/85
Responsible for scheduling, monitoring and inspecting all custom home work from start to finish.
Performed customer service and orientations in a professional manner.
* Homes valued up to $2 million.

U.S. Home, Dallas, TX   3/82-8/83
Superintendent
Budgeted and contracted work on condominium projects.
Scheduled, monitored and inspected all work from start to completion; handled customer orientations.
Processed invoices and directed the service department for the project.

EDUCATION: University of Wisconsin, LaCrosse, WI   1976-1982
Major: Management
Minor: Marketing

U.S. Home, Inc. and Pulte "U", Pulte Home Corp.   1983 and 1989
Completed Management Development Programs.

RICK RODRIGUEZ

2161 W. Schaumburg Road #137
Phoenix, AZ 20193   708/555-9010

CONTRACTOR / CARPENTER

PROFILE:

- More than 12 years in home building, including nine years in all aspects of carpentry for homes valued up to $1 million.

- Supervise and coordinate carpenters in rough framing, interior trim and exterior elevations; maintain excellent quality and work closely with carpenters, builders and subcontractors.

- Perform lumber takeoffs and estimate, purchase, and schedule materials in a cost-effective manner; interpret blueprints and work with building inspectors.

EMPLOYMENT: Sun Contractors, Inc., Schaumburg, IL   1990-Present
Owner / Operator
Responsible for high-quality construction of homes, room additions and numerous remodeling and construction projects.

Trained, supervised and motivated crews of up to 10, including wage determination, assignments, and terminations. Successful experience in all aspects of custom home carpentry, including full contractor duties, with a variety of builders including:
- Carpentry Foreman for Artisan Development Group, Barrington, IL
- Calia Development, Wilmette, IL
  Two homes in South Barrington and Long Grove, IL, valued at $500,000 and $600,000 respectively.
- JWW Builders, Barrington, IL; $900,000 home.
- Affinity Corporation, Arlington Heights, IL; $800,000 home.
- Old Colony Builders, Barrington, IL
  Responsible for 15 different homes valued up to $400,000 each.
- Ivanhoe Development, Mundelein, IL; three homes valued up to $500,000 each.
- Schwall Builders, Northbrook, IL; custom home valued at $650,000.
- Kelgor Construction Company, Barrington, IL; home valued at $600,000.
- Sauers Bros. Const., Laguna Niguel, CA
  One home valued at $1 million and five duplex homes.
- Carpenters, Inc., St. Charles, IL

EDUCATION: Washburne Trade School, Chicago, IL   1980
Completed Journeyman four-year program in three years.
High School Graduate

BERT L. CALL

2145 Devon Avenue
Hanover Park, IL 60103

630-555-5882

COMMERCIAL DIVER

PROFILE:

- ▸ Comprehensive experience in a wide range of technical functions including commercial diving and pipe fitting.

- ▸ Skilled in heavy-duty welding, brazing pipe leaks, penetration diving to 5000 feet and complete ground operations.

- ▸ Proven ability to learn required skills to perform heavy duty work in difficult conditions. Handle equipment management responsibilities such as maintenance and light repair; CPR and First Aid Certified.

EXPERIENCE:

Scott Diving Service, Palatine, IL   6/96–Present
Diving Sub-contractor
Perform all types of underwater operations including construction, debris removal, traveling screen repair and measurements.
Handle penetration work up to 5000 feet; video tape and inspect structures. Document findings with verbal and written reports.
Perform contaminated diving as well as underwater burning to repair and rebuild traveling screens.

H. B. Fuller Tec, Inc., Palatine, IL   11/94–6/96
Materials Handler
Responsible for a wide range of materials management functions such as inventory control, stock organization and stock retrieval.
Handled forklift operations.
Assisted in the development and documentation of ISO 9000 procedures.
Performed quality assurance testing of tile grout to ensure compliance with product requirements.
→ Created, documented and presented a plan to reorganize the inventory storage system. The adopted plan improved inventory accuracy, production line productivity and allowed for proper cycle of dated inventory.

The Tree Company of Barrington, Barrington, IL   10/93–11/94
Ground Man
Managed the set-up, operation and maintenance of all ground equipment, including chippers and shredders, during tree trimming functions.

TECHNICAL TRAINING:

International Commercial Diving Institute, Wilmington, DE
Graduated: Certified Commercial Diver   1996
Certifications in CPR and First Aid.   1995

DANIELA GLOSSLIP

2221 Morningside
Roselle, IL 60172   630/555-0715

COSMETOLOGY / TRAINER

PROFILE:
- ▸ Skilled in all aspects of cosmetology training for groups and individuals, including full program planning, seminars, classroom presentations and student performance reviews.

- ▸ Topics include hair coloring and pressing, skin care, makeup, platform work and aesthetics; well versed in Nexxus and all major cosmetic brands.

- ▸ Handle direct customer service and sales with personal communication skills; fluent in Italian and familiar with Spanish.

EXPERIENCE: <u>Gianni Cosmetics,</u> Bloomingdale, IL   1988-1999
Makeup Artist / Aesthetician
Worked directly with all types of customers and applied cosmetics; trained customers in product lines and applications.

<u>Ippolito School of Cosmetology,</u> Chicago, IL   Intermittent: 1977-1996
Planned and conducted courses in theory, (Milady textbook) as well as basic and advanced courses in permanent waving, color, hair cutting, braiding, air waving, curling iron, skin care, makeup, waxing and aromatherapy.
Trained a wide range of students in product lines and applications, primarily through practical demonstration and supervision of hands-on practice.
* Conducted clinics on sales presentations.
* Supervised all practical work done by students and provided feedback.
* Conducted a lecture and in-salon demonstrations for Nexxus' Aloxxi color, Chicago area, 1996.
* Supervised vocational education field trips and community involvement; prepared students for competitions.
* Prepared students for testing; supervised the mock state board exam; contacted judges and oversaw student competitions.

ACTIVITIES: <u>**Administered classes for Capilustro, Inc**</u>. Worked the Midwest Beauty Trade Show for this Florida wig company. Assisted in training for competition on student and professional levels. Set up and managed a skin care center, performing facials, makeup, aromatherapy and waxing.

EDUCATION: <u>Ippolito School of Cosmetology,</u>   1977
Completed cosmetology and instructor training.

<u>College of Lake County,</u> Grayslake, IL   1996
Completed courses in Basic Computing, Psychology and Spanish.

LYNN KEYTYPE

22549 South Beth
Lombard, IL 60148

630/555-4596

DATA ENTRY / GENERAL OFFICE

PROFILE:

▶ Experienced with proprietary software for data entry and retrieval; update and maintain customer data; familiar with general office equipment including copiers, fax machines and 10-key calculators.

▶ Skilled in customer service and telephone operations; handle customer inquiries and phone presentations in a professional manner.

▶ Trained in various emergency situations as telephone operator; identify problems and coordinate emergency response.

EXPERIENCE: The Signature Group, Elmhurst, IL   1995-1998

Phone Service Representative
Handled both dial-in and dial-out phone contacts with tact and professionalism.
Utilized proprietary software for entering customer information into a computerized database.

→ Performed phone interviews and sales presentations for major clients including Montgomery Wards, CitiBank, Mobile Oil and Fleet.

Ameritech, Lombard, IL   1988-1995

Information Operator
Effectively handled customer inquiries for the information center.
Retrieved phone numbers and addresses from the company database.
Traveled to other company sites to assist with special projects.

→ Provided critical information to emergency service departments as part of 911 operations.
→ Alertly identified and reported emergency situations; calmly talked with victims while coordinating emergency response.

EDUCATION: Earned High School Diploma

MICHAEL TONKA

22637 Fairview Lane
Schaumburg, IL 60193

847-555-5987

DRIVER / CONSTRUCTION EQUIPMENT

EXPERIENCE:
▶ CDL Class A License holder with accident-free record; skilled in driving a wide range of trucks including:
* dump trailers   * redi-mix
* flatbeds   * low boys

▶ Experience in the safe loading and unloading of construction materials.

▶ Update and maintain accurate records of shipments, routes and related costs.

▶ Additional skills in construction, general carpentry and contracting for remodeling, patios and decks.

EMPLOYMENT: Mark Kennedy / WEN Enterprises, Batavia, IL   4/92–Present
Driver
Responsible for the safe driving of various trucks, including flatbeds and dump trailers.
Assist in training new drivers in all company procedures, including updating of daily trip sheets and work orders.
* Duties include loading, delivery and unloading of large sewer pipe, including strapping and chaining.

Newton Construction, Schaumburg, IL   Part-Time/Weekends, 1992–Present
Construction
Perform general construction for room remodeling, concrete and wood patios and decks.

Harry W. Kuhn, West Chicago, IL   1985–1992
Driver
Handled daily driving of redi-mix and dump trucks, delivering gravel and concrete.

B.F. Turgeon, Chicago, IL   1975–1985
Driver
Drove Class A trucks and delivered shipments for numerous companies.

EDUCATION: W.R. Harper College, Palatine, IL   1976–1977
Successful completion of several classes in Culinary Arts and Restaurant Management.

J.B. Conant High School, Hoffman Estates, IL   1974
Graduate

STEVEN B. JOBBS

1019 Woodside Drive
Roselle, IL 60172   630/555-3287

ROAD WORKER / DRIVER

PROFILE:

▸ Proven abilities in road repair including patching with asphalt and concrete; work well with others at all levels of experience.

▸ Experience in heavy lifting and the driving of equipment including Class "C" trucks (licensed), bobcat shovels, snow plows and small steamrollers.

EXPERIENCE:

Illinois Department of Transportation (I.D.O.T.), Schaumburg, IL 9/97-4/99
Highway Maintainer
Responsible for a wide variety of road service functions including road maintenance, damage repairs and snow removal.
Communicated with others in the field to coordinate activities.

Schneider National Carriers, Green Bay, WI   9/92-9/97
Licensed Driver - CDL Class C
Performed all aspects of product delivery and pick-up including customer service, transportation and equipment maintenance.
Served successfully in four divisions with unique responsibilities in each.
→ Received special recognition for Exceptional Customer Service, Safety and Skills.

Specialized Division: **Lead Driver** responsible for all equipment maintenance and repairs.
Worked directly with clients in a professional, personable manner to identify and meet client needs.
→ Recognized as the top producer at Weyerhaeuser.

Truck Rail Division: Transported trailer loads within rail yards throughout Chicago.
Developed contacts and utilized communication skills to improve efficiency.

Dedicated Division: Delivered merchandise from a distribution center to area Target Department Stores.
→ Provided 100% on-time delivery service.

EDUCATION:

International Truck Driving School, Northlake, IL   1992
Completed the Driver Training program.

William Rainey Harper College, Palatine, IL   1991
Successfully completed courses in Psychology and Social Studies.

IZIO SITTARO

2294 Route 53
Addison, IL 60101

630/555-8062

SALES / DRIVER

PROFILE:

▶ Skilled in direct customer service, sales and delivery procedures, including cash collecting, account tracking and status reporting.

▶ Class "C" Driver with an excellent safety record; skilled in driving forklifts and stackers; handle basic data entry and retrieval on computer systems.

▶ Experience with credits, returns and UPS/FedEx shipments; assist in stocking, inventory control and all major warehousing operations.

▶ **Fluent in English, Italian and Spanish;** experience in training and supervising staff in customer service and business procedures.

EXPERIENCE: Calabrese Baking Company, Franklin Park, IL   1995-Present
Driver / Sales Representative
Responsible for the prompt delivery of bread and baked goods to key accounts in the Chicagoland area, including Dominick's and Jewel Food Stores, restaurants and food stands.
Determine efficient routes and drive in a safe manner.
Work closely with customers and update and rotate products on store racks; accurately count and check all items.
Compile and issue customer invoices; handle product returns and credits as required.
→ Collect accurate payments from accounts.
→ Develope a strong client base and constantly seek new accounts.

Turano Baking Company, Bloomingdale, IL   1991-1995
Driver / Production
Duties included mixing and baking for items such as bread and cookies; filled canolli shells and handled a wide range of production duties.
Used kitchen equipment and performed route driving to retail accounts.

Ciao Cafe, Norridge, IL   1992-1995
Manager: 1994-1995 and Owner: 1992-1994
In charge of all operations at this coffee shop, including food purchasing, general accounting, sales and all staff hiring, training and supervision.

Anixter Cable and Wire, Alsip, IL   1989-1991
Shipping / Receiving

EDUCATION: Triton College, River Grove, IL   1992
State of Illinois Sanitation Certified

DeMarinis School, Bari, Italy   **Graduate: High School Equivalent**

THOMAS G. MINO
661 Pinewood Lane
Bloomingale, IL 60108
708/555-3052

CORPORATE DRIVER / COURIER

PROFILE:

▸ More than 10 years as a responsible driver with an accident- and ticket-free record; performs responsibilities accurately and with a high degree of quality.

▸ Dedicated and honest; takes pride in accomplishing tasks beyond expectations.

▸ Enthusiastic with an exceptional attendance record; willingly works overtime and on weekends.

▸ Skilled in interpersonal communications and organization; detail-oriented with excellent time-management skills.

EMPLOYMENT: Greater Illinois Title Company, a spin-off company of Inter County Title, Chicago, IL   1/83-Present
Overnight Messenger
Responsible for twice-per-night transportation of interdepartmental documents to and from 10 locations in the Chicago Metropolitan area. Gather all documents/items from each office and transport them via company van to the proper destination as indicated on the document envelope.
Deliver closing packages, supplies and printed materials accurately and within time frames.

- Determine the most efficient delivery routes based on time and geographic constraints.
- Examine mail pieces for accurate addresses and make corrections as necessary.
- Handle cash, checks and sensitive documents while maintaining confidentiality.
- Promptly deliver outgoing mail to the appropriate U.S. Postal facility.
- Maintain company van and oversee repairs ensuring reliable mechanical and safe operation.
- Ensure all offices are locked after nightly deliveries are completed.
- Provide special overnight delivery service when requested.
- Update manager daily on completed tasks and duties.

EDUCATION: Glenbard South High School, Glen Ellyn, IL, IL   Graduated 1981
GPA: 4.0/4.0 - National Honor Society
College of DuPage, Glen Ellyn, IL   1981-1983
Completed courses in general education

ILYA PATEL

671 Windmill Drive
Hanover Park, IL 60103   708/555-1858

OBJECTIVE: *ELECTRONICS: PROTOTYPE / MECHANICAL ASSEMBLY*
A position utilizing proven technical and training skills.

EXPERIENCE:
- Extensive expertise in building, testing and repairing electronic and mechanical components for telecommunications products.

- Proficient at interpreting and implementing blueprints, schematic drawings, engineering scratch diagrams and Macintosh drawings.

- Effectively work with engineers and managers to develop cost-effective electronic assembly procedures that meet established production deadlines.

EMPLOYMENT: Teradyne Inc., Deerfield, IL   1988-Present
Mechanical Assembler
Personally perform, and train others in technical assembly of telecommunications components: remote measuring unit 2000; test system control units 400, 410, 710 and 720; Telzon block wire-wrapping; artificial lines and voice response systems 400 and 700.

* Selected to provide periodic training on these projects for other employees
* Assist with troubleshooting and repair of machinery.
* Assist other employees with slide line production functions.

Tektronix Portland, OR   1980-1988
Electronic Assembler
Performed wire connection, wire wrapping, board stuffing, hand soldering, clipping and troubleshooting on circuit boards, capacitors, resistors, oscilloscopes and generators.

Kentrox Inc., Portland, OR   1978-1980
Electronic Assembler
Handled board stuffing, soldering, wire wrapping, clipping and repair of various components: two-wire-four-way, two-wire-six-way, four-wire-four-way, four-wire-six-way Telzon blocks; box enclosures and supply units.

EDUCATION: Sardar Patel University, Anand, India   1975-1978

Completed courses in Physics (Electricity), Mathematics, English and Chemistry.

SAMUEL ROBERTS

2229 West North Avenue, #A
Villa Park, IL 60181   630/555-7124

JOURNEYMAN ELECTRICIAN

PROFILE:

▶ Comprehensive experience in the repair and maintenance of motors, control panels and major mechanical and electrical systems, including timers, circuit breakers, feeders, coils and relays.

▶ Experience in commercial and residential electrical wiring, repair and maintenance, as well as mechanical system troubleshooting.

▶ Effectively train staff in system repairs, operations and procedures; utilize multimeters and oscilloscopes; familiar with Windows for data entry and retrieval.

EXPERIENCE:

Steiner Electric, Chicago, IL   1989-9/99
Journeyman Electrician
Responsible for the repair and maintenance of AC, DC, single and 3-phase motors, rewinding, clutches and brakes.
Perform commercial/residential wiring, and mechanical repair of machine shop equipment.
Utilize troubleshooting skills for a broad range of electrical operations and equipment.

Advanced Electric, Addison, IL   1987-1989
Electrician
Utilized a variety of skills in the repair and installation of wiring, as well as winding for electrical motors, breakers and reducers.

New Super Laundry Machine Co., Chicago, IL
Customer Service Manager   1980-1987
Trained and supervised staff in diagnostic techniques and the repair of laundry equipment.
Repaired control panels and acted as company representative on the phone and in the field.
Updated inventories of parts and worked with vendors and suppliers.
* Saved more than $200,000 in equipment costs.

EDUCATION:

DeVry Institute of Technology, Chicago, IL   1987
Received certificate for 2-year program in Digital Electronics.

Coyne American Institute of Technology, Chicago, IL   1979-1980
Electrical Maintenance Diploma
* Dean's List; maintained a 95% GPA.

D.A.V. Inter College, Krakow, Poland   1978
Certificate for courses in physics, chemistry and mathematics.

LYLE W. POLI

2285 Unit A College Drive
Bloomingdale, IL 60108

708/555-4529

ELECTRICIAN

EXPERIENCE:

- More than five years in electrical maintenance and construction for major commercial and residential projects, including wiring and panel installations.

- Skilled in blueprint reading, troubleshooting and general construction for electrical systems to codes and customer specifications.

- Assist in job planning and estimating; work well with foremen, engineers and all other tradesmen.

- Knowledge of lighting and emergency systems, as well as all types of conduit, supplies and testing equipment.

EMPLOYMENT:

Day Electric, Inc., Hanover Park, IL   12/92-5/99
Electrician
Specialized in commercial and residential power distribution and the installation entire systems, primarily for strip malls.
Installed conduit, full service panels and all related wiring to final phase.
* Involved in numerous projects for such customers as Sears Roebuck, Goodyear, Meineke Muffler and two major bakeries.

J.W.P. Gibson Electric Co., Chicago, IL   1/90-11/92
Electrician
Responsible for the installation of wiring, conduit and lighting fixtures, as well as emergency systems.
* Installed systems for the U.S. Post Office, One Schaumburg Place, Sears in Hoffman Estates, an O'Hare Terminal and Marshall Field's flood damage.

Hardt Electric, Chicago, IL   1/88-1/90
Apprentice Electrician
Supervised up to two employees in various shop procedures.
Ordered/purchased parts and materials from numerous vendors.

Cassidy Tire, Chicago, IL   1/86-1/88
Warehouse Manager
Responsible for warehouse operations and order pulling/shipping for 13 stores throughout Chicagoland.

EDUCATION:

Electrical Association   1989
Certificate: Topics included Electricity Theory and Magnetism.
Successful completion of Wireman's Exam   1989
Glenbard North High School, Carol Stream, IL   Graduated 1985

JOHN D. REVVING

22609 Deerfield
Streamwood, IL 60107

630/555-2393

ENGINE REBUILDING / AUTOMOTIVE MECHANIC

EXPERIENCE:

- ▸ Skilled in the total re-building and fabrication of custom and stock engines, rear-ends and gears, as well as blown gas and alcohol motors.

- ▸ Proficient in boring and honing blocks and heads; skilled in the use of lathes, mills, grinders and all general shop equipment.

- ▸ Utilize diagnostic equipment including dynamometers, Bridgeports, CV616 honing machines, Sunnen rod machines and line honing equipment.

- ▸ Perform chassis fabrication and frame work; assemble roll cages and suspensions; proficient in arc, heliarc and gas welding.

- ▸ Worked on a wide range of custom vehicles including:
  Blown gas hydro, 1982; Blown alcohol flat bottom, 1983; a modified production record car, 1982; Top Alcohol Dragster, 1982.

EMPLOYMENT:

<u>J & R Automotive,</u> Streamwood, IL   1/96–Present
Mechanic
Responsible for all aspects of engine rebuilding and repair, and extensive work on high-performance rear-ends and gears.
Rebuild and install manual transmissions for a wide range of classic and late-model cars.
Assist in training and supervising new mechanics.

- * Utilize an all-data computer for part tracking, as well as labor guides and engine specifications.
- * Perform valve jobs and install bronze walls and cylinder heads.

<u>Opel Engineering,</u> Elk Grove, IL
Mechanic / Engine Specialist   1984–1995
Manager / Owner (Prior to selling the company in 1984)   1976–1984
Re-built and/or repaired numerous high-performance engines.

Prior Experience:
<u>Chapman Automobile,</u> Chicago, IL   1971–1976
Head Tune-Up Man
Ran diagnostic tests and dynos; re-built stock and race engines.

EDUCATION: <u>Maine West High School,</u> Des Plaines, IL   Graduate

MARIE R. DANCER

512 Heath Court
Streamwood, IL 60107
630/555-9460

CRUISE SHIP ENTERTAINER

PROFILE:

- ▶ Comprehensive experience and training in dance including Modern, Lyrical, Pop, Ballet, Pointe and Jazz.
- ▶ Quickly learn new dance routines; skilled in modeling for various corporate accounts such as Margies and House of Brides; experience in runway modeling.
- ▶ Willing to travel or relocate for the right opportunity; traveled nationwide for weeks at a time, especially on the east coast.
- ▶ Trained or danced with various professionals including: Waltamore Casey, Van Collins, Jason Myers, Ted Jackson and the Homer Bryant Dance Troupe.

EXPERIENCE:

The Chicago Honeybear Dancers, Chicago, IL — 1995-1997
The Honeybears - Director: Greg Schwartz
As member of the Chicago Honeybears, formerly the Chicago Bear Cheerleaders, performed at numerous shows and fulfilled dance and modeling contracts.

Ted Jackson: Midwest Jazz Troupe, Chicago, IL — 1995-1996
Dancer
Learned numerous routines and performed in various shows in the Midwest.

TRAINING:

Golden's School of Dance, Schaumburg, IL — 1994-1997
Master Classes: Dance Training

Waltmore Casey, Director: Illinois Ballet Academy — 1992-1996
Dance Training

Aragona Dance, Bartlett, IL — 1983-1995
Dance Training

EDUCATION:

Elgin Community College, Elgin, IL — 1997-1998
General Studies

Streamwood High School, Streamwood, IL — Graduated 1997
Completed college prep. courses.
 * **Captain Senior Year: Varsity Pom Pons** — Member: 1994-1997

PERSONAL:

Height: 5'7"	Blue Eyes / Brown Hair	Weight: 120 lbs.
Measurements: 34-24-34	Size 3/5	Born 7/11/79

DAVID A. BERG

224 Gold Circle
Hanover Park, IL 60103   630/555-7278

PROFILE:

FACILITIES / EQUIPMENT MAINTENANCE

▶ Extensive background in the design, production and installation of electronic panels and conveyer equipment; ability to troubleshoot and take corrective action on projects.

▶ Skilled in prevention maintenance activities, including job scheduling, inventory control and contractor supervision; read and interpret blueprints and schematics; specialized knowledge of electrical and electronic systems.

EMPLOYMENT:

Filtran/Division of SPX Corporation, Des Plaines, IL   9/96-2/99
Maintenance Technician
Maintained injection molding equipment, high-speed steel presses and production presses.

Rollex Vinyl Siding, Elk Grove Village, IL   9/94-9/96
Lead Electrician / Maintenance Technician
Maintained and repaired all extrusion equipment and related gear, including computerized PowerTec DC power drives/motors, and American Mapland and Kraus-Maffi PCV extruders and chilled water systems.
Diagnosed and corrected problems accurately and promptly; interfaced with the plant manager, maintenance manager, equipment vendors and maintenance contractors.

→ Visited the Michigan Roll Form plant to gain additional details about the operation and maintenance procedures for this company's equipment.

→ Utilized various tools proficiently, including digital volt meters, air ratchets, AMP probes, thermo-test probes and dial caliber micrometers.

Process Control Technologies (PCT), Addison, IL   8/94-9/94
Lead Electrician
Developed and implemented electrical panels and conveyor equipment; supervised a crew in the operation, maintenance and installation of machinery with AC/DC motors of 120/220/24 volts.

Dynpace, Arlington Heights, IL   1990-1994
Lead Electrician   1/93-8/94
Responsible for the design, development and implementation of electrical panels, including the set-up, maintenance, troubleshooting, reworking and installation of machinery; hired as an Electrician, 8/90.

→ Key team member involved in the development of a prototype shuttle turntable.

U.S. Navy, Alameda, CA   1987-1989
Electrician, Rank E-5
Trained as an electrician for marine systems; supervised electrical tag-out and civilian workers on the overhaul of the USS Carl Vinson; awarded an Armed Forces Expeditionary medal.

EDUCATION:

Southern Illinois University, Carbondale, IL   1985-1987
Received a full scholarship for Technical Theater coursework.
Buffalo Grove High School, Buffalo Grove, IL   Graduated 1985

REGINA ANGLE

230 Wildwood Lane
Hanover Park, IL 60103   630/555-0622

FACILITY AND EQUIPMENT MAINTENANCE

PROFILE:
- Extensive background in all aspects of facility maintenance, and operations management in manufacturing and warehouse environments, with P&L responsibility.
- Skilled in machine setups, equipment repair, cost-effective purchasing, inventory scheduling and shipping/receiving; capacity planning and production cycle control.
- Organize, coordinate and supervise crews in the maintenance of physical structures and mechanical equipment, including prevention maintenance scheduling and on-site troubleshooting; expert in HVAC systems, electrical and plumbing systems.
- Well-versed in production manual/automated machining and assembly equipment installation and operation; interpret blueprints/schematics; effectively work with engineering, quality and operations personnel; fluent in English, Polish and Russian.

EMPLOYMENT: All Star Food, Schaumburg, IL   12/94–Present
Vice President, Production
Manage the full production of packaged health cookies including the mixing, baking, assembly, packaging and purchasing functions; determine production capacity.
Supervise facility maintenance; read and interpret blueprints and schematics.
→ Reduced lead times/run cycles and increased finished goods pallets from 5 to 24 daily.

Harvest Valley Bakery, Spring Valley, IL   8/90-12/93
General Manager
In charge of the setup and operation of this manufacturing plant for LifeStyle USA with outlets in Australia, Canada, England and Japan.
Hired, trained and supervised 40 mixers, packers and machine operators in production, quality control and adherence to customer specifications.
→ Promoted to this position from Maintenance Engineer/Supervisor, 8/90-1/92.

All Star Food, Schaumburg, IL   10/85-8/90
Maintenance Engineer / Supervisor
Supervised crews in plant facility/equipment maintenance and machine setups.
→ Promoted to this position from Mechanic, 12/85-8/87; and Mixer, 10/85-12/85.

OTHER EXPERIENCE: Bednarz Meat and Deli, LaSalle, IL   12/93-Present
Manager
Provide oversight management of this family-owned retail business; train and supervise employees in food preparation, cashiering and customer service.
→ Select, install and maintain capital equipment and negotiate supplier contracts.

EDUCATION: National Education Corporation: Electrical Engineering   1993-Present
Illinois Valley Community College, Oglesby, IL   1993

121

DAVID KINSMAN

1222 Plaza Drive
Fort Wayne, IN 46806

219/555-2894

OBJECTIVE: A position utilizing skills in heavy equipment repair, machine shop procedures and staff management.

EXPERIENCE:

▶ Skilled in all aspects of equipment maintenance and repair, as well as inventory control, purchasing, shop procedures and general management.

▶ Familiar with parts fabrication and all major shop equipment including lathes, grinders, mills, drill presses and arc, mig and gas welders.

▶ Effectively train work crews in on-site and shop repair of cranes, (25-225 ton) backhoes, excavators, forklifts and boomtrucks.

▶ Skilled in reading blueprints and schematics, as well as magnet/general setups, shearing machines and sheet metal work.

▶ Experience in the complete overhaul of diesel and gas engines and hydraulic, electrical and mechanical systems; hands-on experience with all major brands and systems including:
  - American Machine, Prentice (and related computer systems), Daewoo, Bucyrus-Erie, Heine-Warner Machine and Caterpillar and Cummins engines.
  - Link Belt: eight years of experience with LS, UC, HSP, LS48 and LS418 models.
  - Forklift models including Clark, Tow Motor and Yale.
  - Electrical, commercial/household: 110, 220, 3-phase.
  - Automotive/construction: 12-24 volt and millivolt.

EMPLOYMENT: B and W Equipment Company, Inc., Fort Wayne, IN   1988-Present
Shop Foreman / Service Technician
Responsible for training, scheduling and supervising a team of eight employees in heavy equipment troubleshooting and maintenance.
Handle direct customer service and communications to quickly solve equipment problems.
Travel to major construction sites for repairs.
  - Management duties include inventory control, parts purchasing, warranty claim processing and invoicing.

CERTIFICATES: Certified in Prentice Hydraulic Machines
Certified in Daewoo Hydraulic Excavators and the Mega 400 Loader
Certified for completion of Series 671 Diesel Overhaul Training.

EDUCATION: Ivy Technical School, Fort Wayne, IN   **Graduate:** 1990

MARK A. TORCH
27W22 Sycamore Lane
West Chicago, IL 60185
708/555-3877

OBJECTIVE: *FIREFIGHTER:* A position as full-time or paid-on-call Firefighter where solid training and skills would be utilized.

EXPERIENCE:
- **Certified EMT-A**, including hands-on experience in emergency situations; trained in basic life support and extrications.

- **Certified Fire Apparatus Engineer; Certificate** in Fire Ground Tactics and Fire Alarms and Systems.

- Trained in fire codes and regulations for buildings and sprinkler systems, and in fire science apparatus and fire spreading in various types of buildings.

- Knowledge of sprinkler installations and plumbing/building systems, including water connections and sewer systems.

EMPLOYMENT: Globe Plumbing, Inc., West Chicago, IL   6/85-Present
Plumber / Engineer
Perform engineering and installation for piping in industrial, commercial, educational and correctional facilities.
Layouts include sewer, water, process and chemical piping.
Utilize a transit to survey grades as needed.
Pro-Care Ambulance Service, Roselle/Elgin, IL   10/94-3/95
Shift Supervisor
Involved in a wide range of emergency situations including auto accidents, prompt medical care/patient stabilizing and transportation to hospitals.

VOLUNTEER: Lombard Fire Protection District, Lombard, IL   1/94
Volunteer / Firefighter Trainee
Assisted in ambulance calls and gained direct experience as EMT-A.

EDUCATION: College of DuPage, Glen Ellyn, IL
Trained in subjects listed above, as well as fire prevention and protection techniques and equipment.
Trained in Hydraulics for FAE Certificate, 5/95.
Additional Education in Engineering and Calculus.
Courses included Fire Prevention II, Emergency Medical Technician, Building Construction, and Fire Science Apparatus.

MICHAEL D. FLYER

6601 N. Cuyler 3rd Floor
Oak Park, IL 60302   708/555-8005

OBJECTIVE: To rechannel my extensive customer service and communications skills into a position as a Flight Attendant.

PROFILE:
- Comprehensive experience in effective customer service and business administration, including communications and problem-solving with tact and professionalism.
- Familiar with human resource functions and staff development; plan and conduct meetings and staff training in professional customer relations, computer systems and full office support.
- Utilize/streamline computer systems including MS Word, Excel, Productivity Point and EMH networks for email.

EMPLOYMENT: Elmhurst Memorial Hospital, Elmhurst, IL
Assistant Manager: Registration and Scheduling Services 5/96-Present
Perform monthly staff meetings and implement new policies and procedures; constantly update staff on changes to systems and operations. Update and process payroll on a bi-weekly basis.
Conduct staff performance reviews; draft memos and submit general notices.
- Computer functions include managing user codes, testing and upgrades.
- Developed and implemented an Accountlink optical imaging system.
- Created a new hire packet and developed a computer training guide, as well as a master binder outlining insurance benefits.
- Conducted training of numerous off-site staff personnel in patient registration and related procedures. Attended Continuous Improvement Training.
- Act as United Way representative and the Infection Control Manager.
- Developed a strong team environment among all front-house staff.

Registrar,   5/95-5/96:
Admitted all types of patients to the hospital; secured medical insurance documentation and verified coverage. Registered patients for outpatient testing and the emergency room. Acted as information/reception desk operator: greeted patients and provided directions and customer service.

Old Kent Bank, Lombard, IL   3/92-5/95
Customer Service Representative / Teller
Handled direct customer service and cash/non-cash transactions in a professional manner; assisted customers with CDs, checking/savings accounts and credit cards.
- Completed extensive training in directed customer service, telephone skills, sales, positive image and managing difficult situations.

EDUCATION: Elmhurst College, Elmhurst, IL
B.S. Degree, Major: Health Management   Graduated 2/96
Minor: Sociology   * Dean's List

ANNA L. NIKI

44276 Raleigh Court #202
Glendale Heights, IL 60139

708/555-9257

OBJECTIVE:	**Flight Attendant:** A position utilizing customer service and communication skills.
EXPERIENCE:	■ Proven abilities as Flight Attendant, including food service and customer relations, waitressing, sanitation and the preparation of work stations. ■ Trained in pre- and in-flight procedures and safety; fluent in Spanish.

EMPLOYMENT:

American Airlines/American Eagle, Chicago, IL 7/93-Present
Flight Attendant
Responsible for all aspects of customer service and in-flight safety.
Successful completion of four week's training in a wide range of safety procedures, including general first aid, emergency exit use, mouth-to-mouth resuscitation, the Heimlich maneuver and water, fire and hijacking emergencies.

Truffles Grove Restaurant, Itasca, IL Part-Time, 11/92-Present
Waitress
Responsible for professional serving of food and liquor to a wide range of customers.
Communicate with customers and answer questions on menu items; handle a full range of side work and cleanup duties.

Dearborn Const. & Development, Roselle, IL 11/90-6/93
Secretary / Bookkeeper
Communicated daily with customers and provided information on account status, products and services.
Processed AP/AR, cash receipts and monthly/quarterly financial statements.

Indian Lakes Resort, Bloomingdale, IL 1/90-11/90
Front Desk Clerk and Reservationist
Performed daily check-in and check-out for customers; assigned rooms and solved problems in a professional manner.
Arranged transportation for customers and updated and maintained their accounts via computer terminal.

Carson Pirie Scott, Bloomingdale, IL 7/89-1/90
Sales Representative

EDUCATION: Palm Beach Junior College, Lake Worth, FL Business Courses, 1987-1989

Cardinal Gibbons High School., Ft. Lauderdale, FL Graduated 1987

PERSONAL: Excellent Health; Non-Smoker; Willing to Relocate.

BETH A. SLICER

226 Garden Circle Drive #6
Streamwood, IL 60107   708/555-3857

OBJECTIVE: **Food Service**
A position utilizing skills in food preparation and customer service.

EXPERIENCE:
- More than nine years in food service operations including creative, specialty food preparation and personalized customer service.

- Assist in staff hiring, training and supervision; organize work schedules, purchasing, inventories and stock rotation.

EMPLOYMENT: Cub Foods, Naperville, IL   1/88-Present
Deli Clerk   5/92-Present
Assist in supervising up to six employees in creative food preparation, assembly and presentation, as well as customer service and sales activities. Update and maintain inventories of food and kitchen equipment and supplies; assist in timely stock ordering with vendors and suppliers. Responsible for sales and answering customer questions related to food storage and preparation.
* Ensure excellent sanitation of all equipment.

Seafood Clerk - Lombard Location   1/88-5/92
Effectively hired, trained and supervised up to six employees in seafood preparation, sales and direct customer service.
* Chosen to train for management position.

Cee Bee's Finer Foods, Glen Ellyn, IL   1/87-1/88
Deli Manager (smaller scale store)
Involved in cost-effective food and equipment purchasing with numerous vendors and suppliers.
Hired, trained and supervised staff in all deli procedures; maintained inventories and assisted in ordering and inventory control.
* Trained for management position.

Supreme Lobster, Palatine, IL   1/85-1/87
Chef's Assistant
Responsibilities included product presentation and preparation.
Hired and trained staff in inventory control and stock ordering.
* Trained under chef's supervision in gourmet cooking with fish.

Cub Foods, Arlington Heights, IL   8/84-1/85
Seafood Manager
Performed inventory control and maintained product freshness and presentation.
* Ensured high standards of customer satisfaction and service.

EDUCATION: Buffalo Grove High School, Buffalo Grove, IL   Graduated 1983

PHIL ZURAWSKI

1228 Winder Lane #6
Cordova, TN 38018

901/555-3229

FORESTRY

PROFILE:

▸ Comprehensive experience/education in a wide range of forestry applications including reforestation, cruising, marking, inventory and land management.

▸ Detailed knowledge of all regional tree species; proven ability to set and meet challenging objectives.

▸ Utilize proficient communication, negotiation and interpersonal skills to coordinate activities and work effectively in a team environment.

EXPERIENCE:

Spray-Tech, Inc. / Sears Home Improvement, Memphis, TN
Outside / In-home Sales Representative 1997-Present
Handle all sales and marketing functions, including presentations and needs assessment for home improvement products such as vinyl siding, patio doors and windows.
→ Close 27% of prospective clients.

Pomeroy & McGowin Forestry Company, Monticello, AK
Forestry Assistant / Forester 1995-1996 and 1997
Responsible for all aspects of forestry including cruising, marking and reforestation.
Conducted inventory by species; identified and marked trees ready to cut and sell.
Surveyed lands to check for various natural problems such as defects and disease.
→ Planned and prescribed controlled fires to manage lands; stimulate tree growth, prevent wild fires and reduce timber litter.
→ Coordinate controlled fire activities with other personnel in the field.
→ Established, brushed, blazed and marked land lines.

University of Tennessee, Dendrology Department, Knoxville, TN
Forestry Assistant / Work-Study 1996-1997
Performed a wide range of tasks and projects designed by the department faculty for teaching entry-level forestry students.

Jack D. Branch, Jr. and Company, Consulting Foresters, Collierville, TN
Forestry Assistant 1989-1995
Cruised and marked trees for selective harvesting.

EDUCATION:

University of Tennessee, Knoxville, TN
Bachelor of Science Degree in Forestry 1997
→ Assembled a complete collection of bark samples from every tree species native to Tennessee, now in use as an instructional tool for forestry students.

MAX HEDLIFT

22298 Meadow Lane
Carol Stream, IL 60188

708/555-1786

OBJECTIVE: **FORK LIFT DRIVER / WAREHOUSING**

EXPERIENCE:
- Proven abilities in stocking, order-picking, shipping and receiving.

- Skilled in safe forklift driving and warehouse operations; handle order expediting of electronics and fragile equipment.

- Experience in worker training and supervision; knowledge of general bookkeeping and business administration; self-motivated and energetic.

EMPLOYMENT: **Apple Computer, Inc.,** Through ADIA Services, Itasca, IL   7/92-Present
Permanent / Lead Warehouseman
Responsible for safe forklift driving, order-picking and stocking of computer equipment at this major warehouse.
Perform loading/unloading of trucks on a daily basis.
Assist in cross-training employees in order-picking, stocking and packing for international shipment.

   * Recognized as Employee of the Month, 2/93, for prompt, safe work.

Max and Sons Foodservice, Addison, IL   1991-1992
Manager / Owner
Involved in the setup and operation of this company.
Assisted in the training and supervision of 15 employees in the delivery of fresh and frozen foods to restaurants and stores.
Handled all budgets and general bookkeeping.

Tower Contractors, Addison, IL   1989-1990
Laborer
Responsible for the custom application of aluminum siding.

EDUCATION: Davea Career Center   1991-1992
Trained in computer repair and maintenance.

Austin High School, Chicago, IL   Graduated 1989

DAVID A. MELTER

6N817 Longacre
St. Charles, IL 60175

630/443-4092

FOUNDRY OPERATIONS

PROFILE:

- ▶ Extensive background in foundry procedures and metallurgy, including experience in machining and assembly for a wide range of products.
- ▶ Assist in product development and post-sale customer service; familiar with hiring, training and scheduling work crews.
- ▶ Well-versed in manufacturing processes and equipment; read and interpret blueprints to comply with close-tolerance, industry and customer specifications; develop a strong rapport with customers for solid business relationships.

EMPLOYMENT:

Rice Lake Weighing, Rice Lake, WI   8/94–1/00
A privately held manufacturer of replacement mechanical parts for industrial scales.
Casting Operator, Machining Operations
Mill raw castings received from such foundries as Waupaca and Badger, in accordance with blueprint specifications and weights by industry.
Utilize, setup and maintain a variety of machining tools, including drill presses, lathes, hydraulic presses and Milwaukee Kearney Trecker single/dual spindle milling machines.
- → Train new employees in machining/assembly operations, product specifications, equipment maintenance and technical support.
- → *Crew member, construction project*: built rough deck platforms to hold the electronic equipment used to program machining specifications.

Carpet Town, Rice Lake, WI   1994–1996
Sales Associate, Part-time

Davenport Agency/American Family Insurance Co., Chetek, WI   1980–1994
Manager / Insurance Agent
Marketed and sold multiple-line commercial and residential insurance, with PandL responsibility for account acquisition and maintenance.
- → Received an award for the highest life insurance sales nationally.

Sir Anthony James, Rice Lake, WI   1975–1980
General Manager / Owner
Directed sales and office staff in marketing, sales and business operations of this franchise selling home fire alarm systems and appliances.

COMMUNITY SERVICE:

Dean's List Big Band/University of Wisconsin affiliation   1966–1997
Musician, Trumpet

MILITARY SERVICE:

U.S. Navy, Norfolk, VA   1971–1974
Musician / 3rd Class: completed the U.S. Naval School of Music coursework.

EDUCATION:

University of Wisconsin Technical College, Rice Lake, WI
A.A. degree in Marketing

RETT MOWER

22816 Oriole Drive
Streamwood, IL 60107

708/555-4226

OBJECTIVE: **Grounds Maintenance**
A position where grounds keeping, building maintenance and carpentry skills will be utilized.

EXPERIENCE:
- ▶ More than three years in grounds keeping and building maintenance including all-season work; experience in lawn work and snow removal.

- ▶ More than eight years in carpentry work and building maintenance; experience in drywall, taping and painting.

- ▶ Skilled in use of bobcat, grasshopper mower, John Deere tractor with snowblower and 4x4 truck with attached plow; knowledgeable in light plumbing and electrical work.

EMPLOYMENT: Building By Beto, Inc., Bartlett, IL 4/92-Present
Carpenter
Perform carpentry work including drywall, taping and painting.
Assist in plumbing and electrical work.
Maintained exterior of buildings including repair and painting.

Streamwood Park District, Streamwood, IL Winter 1990-1995
Snow Removal - Part Time
On call for snow removal utilizing pickup trucks with 6-foot plow blades.

Jenson Windows, Elgin, IL 4/91-9/91
Carpenter
Removed commercial windows and installed new windows.

PERSONAL: Completed an OSHA Safety Course.
Member of Carpenter's Union Local 839 of Hoffman Estates.
Active member of the Streamwood Moose Lodge #2055.
Former Board Member and Coach of the Streamwood Little League.
Currently Umpire for the Streamwood Little League.

EDUCATION: J.B. Conant High School, Hoffman Estates, IL
Graduate 1990

KATHY WALTERS
7733 White Oak Drive
Roselle, IL 60172
708/555-6770

OBJECTIVE: A position as Hostess, where professional skills would be utilized.

EXPERIENCE:
- Proven abilities in customer service and staff training in fine dining and resort restaurants.
- Assist in record keeping, inventory control and general bookkeeping; experience with the Squirrel computer system.
- Handle telephone communications, reservations and banquet coordination in a professional manner.

EMPLOYMENT: Indian Lakes Resort, Bloomingdale, IL   1990-Present
Hostess
Responsible for up to 20 servers at the Frontier Grill/Cafe and On-The-Pond, a fine dining restaurant, with a combined capacity of 340.
Perform monthly inventories of supplies and equipment, including glassware and wine.
Utilize the Squirrel system for bill processing.
Handle virtually all telephone reservations for large and small groups.
* Perform light typing and assist in payroll processing.
* Supervise the setup of daily buffets.

Jimmy's Cock and Bull Restaurant, West Chicago, IL   1989-1990
Manager / Hostess
Trained/supervised and scheduled up to 16 servers in customer relations and cashiering.
Handled extensive billing, check writing and accounts payable.

TPI Plumbing Co., Villa Park, IL   1987-1989
Administrative Assistant
Duties included correspondence typing, bill processing and telephone communications with customers and suppliers.
Performed a wide range of general office functions.

Drake Hotel, Oak Brook, IL   1979-1982
Reservationist / Corporate Relations
Worked closely with hundreds of businesses to arrange VIP accommodations for executives and travelers.
Handled all communications in a professional, yet personalized manner.

EDUCATION: Wright Jr. College, Chicago, IL   Various Business courses.

High School Graduate

COMMUNITY SERVICES: **Vice President:** Lake Park Hockey Club   1986-1988
Supervised fund raisers and sporting events.

PERRY VASQUEZ

4249 Sebring Circle
Elgin, IL 60120

847/555-9314

HVAC REPAIR AND MAINTENANCE

PROFILE:

▶ Hands-on training in HVAC system repair, troubleshooting and maintenance, covering heating systems, air conditioning, electronics and refrigeration.

▶ Diagnose and repair problems with oil, gas and high-efficiency furnaces.

▶ **Certified** by Rheem for 90+ efficiency furnaces and the True Blue furnace; **Certified** by the EPA to handle refrigerants.

▶ Experience in direct customer service, job scheduling and general bookkeeping; background in staff training, supervision and motivation.

EDUCATION: <u>ETI: Environmental Technical Institute</u>, Itasca, IL   10/97-10/98

HVAC Certificate
Numerous classes and lab training, including:

* House Wiring
* Electric Heating Systems
* Gas Heating Systems
* Steam Heating Systems
* Advanced Electricity & Low Voltage Wiring
* High Efficiency Heating Systems & Air Filtering Devices
* Sheet Metal & Associated Equipment
* Pipe Sizing, Cutting, Threading & Soldering/Brazing
* Air Conditioning & Refrigeration Systems

* Basic Electricity
* Oil Heating Systems
* Hydronic Heating Systems

EMPLOYMENT: <u>Jewel Food Stores</u>, Lisle, IL   10/78-Present
Produce Manager
Responsible for direct customer service and sales support, to determine and meet the customer's needs.
Update and maintain weekly job schedules and write daily orders for vendors and suppliers.
Process daily and weekly books.

→ Consistently exceed all sales records and earnings in the department.
→ Completed supervisory training levels 1,2 and 3.
→ Qualified to manage the entire store in absence of the Store Manager.

THOR T. FURNACE

12267 Crabtree Lane
Bartlett, IL 60103   708/555-1434

OBJECTIVE: **HVAC MANAGEMENT**
A position where supervisory skills and experience in the HVAC industry will be utilized.

PROFILE:
- ▸ Hands-on training in HVAC system troubleshooting, repair and maintenance of air conditioning, heating systems, and electronics.

- ▸ Experience in direct customer service, purchasing and order expediting, and negotiating with vendors; organize all aspects of business ownership including general accounting, and invoicing.

- ▸ Skilled in hiring, training, and motivating technicians.

EXPERIENCE: AFT Heating and Air Conditioning, Wheeling, IL   5/86-Present
Owner / Operator
Created and set up this company to provide service, retro-fit, and new construction for residential and commercial North Shore area of Chicago.
Plan and develop sales/market penetration strategies; forecast sales.
Responsible for hiring, training, and scheduling of service technicians, and subcontractors.
Work directly with vendors on system designs, delivery time frames, and pricing.
Handle direct customer contact and quality assurance.
- → Increased business to more than 1,700 accounts through personal sales.
- → Completed multi-million dollar installations of new HVAC construction for the Optima Company, the J.S. James Co., and Swiss Valley Dairy, Inc.

R. H. Witt, Glenview, IL   1982-5/86
Service Manager
Handled job scheduling, stocking, and installation of HVAC systems.
Responsible for accounts receivable and invoicing.

EDUCATION: Ferris State University, Ferris, MI   1995
Certificate of Completion
Refrigerant Transition and Recovery Certifications, Type I and II

Wood Heating Education and Research Foundation, Mt. Pleasant, IA   1995
Certificate of Completion
Wood Burning Fireplace Installation

Refrigeration Service Engineers Society / Commonwealth Edison   1989
Completed Heat Pump Training Course

ITT Technical Institute, Indianapolis, IN   1977
Air Conditioning, Heating and Refrigeration Certificate

Paxton Community High School, Paxton, IL   1976

WILLIAM M. SHIPPER

22119 12th Avenue
Bartlett, IL 60103   708/555-7798

OBJECTIVE: **IMPORT / EXPORT AND FREIGHT OPERATIONS**

EXPERIENCE:
- Proven abilities in freight dispatching and routing, including responsibility for import/export operations and fleet coordination.

- Skilled in freight consolidation and air and ocean transport; strong knowledge of customs, tariffs, carriers, rates, services and routes.

- Handle all NVOCC department functions, as well as data entry/retrieval on computerized systems; file tariffs with the FMC.

EMPLOYMENT: Nettles and Co., Inc., Elk Grove Village, IL   5/91-Present
Export Specialist
In charge of all NVOCC operations and the coordination of fabric shipments via ocean carriers from the Southern and Northern U.S. Involved in all aspects of ocean export documentation and bookings. Organize container movement and LCL with co-loaders. Perform ocean consolidations and file tariffs with the FMC.
* Work extensively with Intertrans, Ltd, Barking, England.

W.E.S.T. Forwarding Services, Elk Grove Village, IL   5/88-5/91
Ocean Freight Consolidator
Responsible for all phases of NVOCC and duties listed above.

A.C. Express, Elk Grove Village, IL   Part time 7/88-1/89
Supervisor
Effectively trained and managed five drivers and four employees in office support.
Organized trucking operations for virtually all types of outgoing domestic freight.

Expeditors International, Wood Dale, IL   8/87-5/88
International Export Documentation Agent
Performed all aspects of export and professional customer service.

MSAS Cargo International, Des Plaines, IL   4/81-8/87
Export Agent
Utilized a Sperry Univac computer for a wide range of export activities.

Union Air Transport, Bensenville, IL   11/76-4/81
Export Agent / Supervisor

EDUCATION: Manatee Junior College, Bradenton, FL   Two Year's Courses

Hartford Airline Personnel School, CT   Graduate

ROBERT WOK

2341 Custer Court
Fox Lake, IL 60022   708/555-4739

KITCHEN MANAGER

PROFILE:
- ▶ Experience as Sous Chef and Line Supervisor including menu pricing, continental cuisine and customer service; train and supervise staff for peak performance.
- ▶ Proven abilities in all kitchen operations, including food preparation, cooking and cost-effective purchasing and inventory control.
- ▶ Sanitation Certified, State of Illinois, 1991; background in catering, line cooking and banquet/kitchen coordination.

EMPLOYMENT: Key Colony Inn, Key Colony Beach, FL   10/94–5/99
Sous Chef
Responsible for daily food preparation, line opening and sanitation at this restaurant rated #1 in the Middle Keys by The People's Choice Awards.
- → Handled menu preparation, inventory, quality control and cleanup.
- → Assisted in banquet preparation, specializing in pasta and sauces.
- → Worked pantry and broiler stations.

Holiday Inn, Marathon, FL   10/93–10/94
Chef, Royal Pelican Restaurant
Transferred by Embassy Suites; successfully brought hotel restaurant to a full-service facility providing breakfast, lunch and dinner.
- → Implemented new menu; hired, trained, scheduled and supervised staff.
- → Set up banquet operation and implemented procedures for purchasing, inventory and quality control; handled purveyor and vendor relations.

Embassy Suites Hotel, Schaumburg, IL   5/93–10/93
Sous Chef
Prepared and coordinated banquets for up to 800 guests.
Supervised line staff and created daily specials; ensured excellent product quality.

Wyndham Hotel, Naperville, IL   10/91–5/93
Night Supervisor/Lead Cook
Responsible for the supervision of four employees in evening kitchen operations.
- → Achieved Wyndham's #1 ranking for food quality.

EDUCATION: College of DuPage, Glen Ellyn, IL   1/92–5/92
Completion of courses towards A.S. Degree include Culinary Arts, Nutrition, Menu Design and Food Purchasing.

Cooking and Hospitality Institute of Chicago, Chicago, IL
Certificate: Professional Cooking,   1992

MICHAEL J. SCAPER

2285 Wildwood Drive
Streamwood, IL 60107   630/555-2097

OBJECTIVE: **LANDSCAPING**
A position where lawn/garden sales and landscaping field experience would be of value.

PROFILE:
- ▶ Experience and training in the decorative planting and maintenance of residential and commercial gardens and grounds.
- ▶ Train, supervise and evaluate new employees in lawn mowing, fertilizer application, soil testing, seeding, starter planting, pruning, weed control and disease/insect problem resolution.

EMPLOYMENT: Trugreen / Chemlawn, Schaumburg, IL   1986-Present
Tree & Shrub Specialist   3/91-Present
In charge of the Tree & Shrub Division, with responsibility for field operations in a suburban territory.
Handle difficult customer problems for all routes; resolve discrepancies and respond to inquiries about disease, insect and weed control for full customer satisfaction.

Lawn Care Specialist   3/86-3/91
Responsible for a daily residential lawn care route schedule, including fertilizer applications, weed/disease control, inspections and homeowner instruction.
Maintained a truck and all equipment in operating condition.
→ Completed workshops on diseases, insects and fertilization applications.

Kmart Corporation, Elk Grove Village, IL   10/96-Present
Sales Associate, Part-time
Sell, promote and merchandise lawn and garden products to retail customers. Respond to customer product inquiries and assist in sales promotions, stock replenishment, in-store display setups and inventory control.

Wal-Mart, Streamwood, IL   10/91-4/96
Sales Associate, Part-time
Rotated among departments to replenish shelves, count inventories, set up displays and assist customers with inquiries; unloaded and received goods on the night shift.

Sears, Woodfield Mall, Schaumburg, IL   9/81-4/91
Sales, Hardware Department, Part-time

Direct Marketing Technology, Schaumburg, IL   1981-1986
Printer, 5/81-9/84: generated laser prints of advertising flyers and brochures; monitored job schedules and determined priority based on job requirements.

EDUCATION: William Rainey Harper College, Palatine, IL   1980-1982
A.A. degree in Computer Science

St. Viator High School, Arlington Heights, IL   Graduated 1980

DONALD H. TRAINMAN

2201 Pleasant Place   Residence: 630/555-7954
Streamwood, IL 60107   Pager: 708/555-0079

OBJECTIVE: **LOCOMOTIVE ENGINEER**

LOCATIONS:

▶ Terminal   Zone
    Bensenville   F
    Milwaukee   C

PROFILE:

▶ Experience in virtually all aspects of road and yard operations; completed Conductor School; military service in Vietnam; knowledge of Lotus 1-2-3 for Windows; Illinois class "C" driver license.

▶ Proficient analytical, technical and mechanical skills gained from 25 years in the railroad industry; communicate effectively to identify and resolve problems.

EMPLOYMENT:

Canadian Pacific Railway/SOO Line, HQ, St. Paul, MN   1/96–Present
Conductor, Bensenville, IL
Operate thru-freight and way-freight trains on the Bensenville/Davenport line, in full compliance with operating rules, state/local regulations and interstate laws.
Document run statistics; prepare reports such as train delay and wheel reports.

→ *Yard Service experience includes*: hump operations/transfer jobs to other railroads.

Union Pacific Railroad, Chicago, IL   1971–1995
(formerly Chicago & Northwestern Railroad)
Supervisor, Timekeeping Department   10/93–10/95
Responsible for all payroll and timekeeping functions for train and engine personnel. Trained and supervised 14 employees.

Office Manager, Credit & Collections Department   9/88–10/93
Supervised a staff of four in cash transactions, payables and aging receivables.

→ Directly handled funds transfers between railroad companies for interline settlements.

Supervisor, Accounts Payable Department   10/78–9/88
Performed general ledger maintenance and processed payments.

→ Orchestrated the Department conversion from UNIVAC to a PC-based LAN system.

Commuter Services Representative   10/72–10/78
Handled passenger inquiries and complaints accurately, promptly and tactfully; inspected commuter stations for adherence to safety, cleanliness, service operations and maintenance policies and standards.
Worked closely with the Engineering Department to resolve problems.

→ Promoted to this position from **Clerk** in 1971.

MILITARY:

U.S. Marine Corps, Camp Pendleton, CA/Vietnam   1967–1971
Rank: Corporal

→ Instructor in truck driving.

TRAINING:

Numerous seminars/courses completed include:
Accounting I&II and Tax Accounting, Northwestern University

EDUCATION: Lane Technical High School, Chicago, IL

ED GRINDER

2315 Norridge Lane
Hoffman Estates, IL 60194

847/555-3890

OBJECTIVE: *MACHINIST:*
A position utilizing skills in manual or CNC machining and programming.

PROFILE:
- ► Read and interpret blueprints to adhere with close-tolerance (.0002) machining; well-versed in metrics and QC/SPC; utilize precision hand tool and measuring equipment; fluent in English, Polish and Russian.
- ► Graduated from Business Industrial Resources Training Center; Mazak CNC Operations & Setup, Mazak CNC Part Programming, CNC Lathe & Mills Operations, Programming with Fanuc Control, Quality Control & Blueprint Reading and Principles of CAD/CAM classes.
- ► Thorough knowledge of manual/computerized machining equipment including Mazatrol and Fanuc Control machining & turning centers; fabricate tool and die molds to manufacture Mazatrol and Fanuc Control equipment.

EMPLOYMENT: A. M. Precision Machining, Inc., Elk Grove, IL   1997-Present
Machinist, Milling Department
Responsible for the set-up and programming of horizontal and vertical machining centers with 3 and 5 axis Fanuc control.

Smalley Steel Ring Company, Wheeling, IL   1991-1997
Machinist, Seal Division
Performed setups/teardowns, tolerance pre-sets, operator maintenance and troubleshooting for the machining of seal rings for this contractor to biomedical, aerospace and military accounts.
- → Worked extensively with mills, lathes and grinders.
- → Rotated between Seal Division and the Retaining and Wave Spring Department.

The Spin Smith Corporation, Wood Dale, IL   1989-1991
Machinist, Tool Room
Milled soft/hard steel, including aluminum and stainless, to manufacture parts for lighting OEMs, utilizing various types of mills, grinders and lathes.

TRAINING: Courses completed include:
Quality Control/SPC, Safety on the Job, Jewelry Design/Production, CNC Lathe & Mill Operations and Programming with Fanuc & Mazatrol Control.

EDUCATION: W.R. Harper College, Palatine, IL
Completed courses in manual machining and CNC setup/programming.

WSOWRIR Engineering Technology College, Poland   1980

VAL RIPKEN

2263 Daisy Lane, Unit 113
Roselle, IL 60172

630/555-1509

MACHINE SETUP / OPERATIONS

PROFILE:

▶ Extensive background in all aspects of job shop machining, including setup, drilling, milling, laser cutting/marking and lapping/fine grinding.

▶ Read and interpret blueprints; machine within close tolerances to meet strict job and quality specifications.

▶ <u>Utilize and operate a variety of machines, equipment and tools:</u>

  - Multiple spindle machines
  - Davenport machines
  - Surface grinders
  - Lathes
  - Rotary transfer machines
  - Gauges/Micrometers
  - Mechanical tools

▶ Machine steel, aluminum and brass fittings for parts and components ordered by OEMs in electrical, automotive and construction industries; ability to process up to 500,000 parts per order.

▶ Fluent in English and Spanish; willing to relocate.

EMPLOYMENT: **Machine Setup Operator** at various locations:

<u>L.D. Redmer Screw Products</u>, Inc., Bensenville, IL	3/91-Present
<u>Norton Plastic Performance</u>, Elk Grove Village, IL	6/88-12/90
<u>Avanti Engineering</u>, Bensenville, IL	2/87-4/88
<u>K.K. Screw Products</u>, Itasca, IL	4/83-1/87

EDUCATION: <u>Washburne Trade School</u>, Chicago, IL
Two-year Certificate, received 1983

JOHN P. WRENCH

3400 Conway Bay
Roselle, IL 60172

630/555-0869

MAINTENANCE MECHANIC

PROFILE:

▶ Perform cost-cutting modifications that improve safety and boost machine productivity. Troubleshoot systems accurately and repair breakdowns quickly to maintain operating efficiency.

▶ Completed the advanced, two-day Omron PLC Programming course.

▶ Proven abilities in a wide range of technical skills including:

Blueprint reading	Mig, Arc, Gas Welding
Hydraulics	3-phase electric motors
Sheet metal layout, fabrication	480V AC-24V DC
Air compressors	AC & DC drives

EXPERIENCE:

Knight Plastics, Arlington Heights, IL   2/98-Present
Maintenance Mechanic
Responsible for all aspects of troubleshooting and repair of a wide range of machines such as Injection Molders, Decorating Machines, Vacuum Loaders and Assembly Machines.
Planned and implemented alterations for added safety, to improve operator ergonomics and increase machine productivity.

SPX Filtran, Des Plaines, IL   1997-1998
Maintenance Mechanic (Third Shift)
Performed maintenance and repair of semi-automated equipment, PLC controlled assembly lines, and handled all duties similar to those listed above under Knight Plastics.

American Flange & Mfg. Company, Carol Stream, IL   1996-1997
Maintenance Mechanic
Responsible for the set-up and performance of preventative maintenance on a range of machines such as Bliss Punch Presses, Kaufman Mill & Thread machines and Cincinnati Injection Molders. Handled the fabrication of equipment modifications to upgrade systems.

U.S. Navy   1992-1996
Hull Maintenance Technician / Ship Fitter
Conducted a wide range of ship repairs in accord with OSHA and NAVOSH regulations. Performed welding, cutting and grinding on materials such as carbon steel, stainless steel, aluminum and copper-nickel.

EDUCATION:

College of DuPage, Glen Ellyn, IL
→ Successfully completed classes in Schematic Interpretation and Basic Electricity.

MARVIN A. MAKER

2277 Ontarioville Road #309D
Hanover Park, IL 60103   708/555-7385

OBJECTIVE: **Manufacturing / Engineering**
A position where solid technical skills would be utilized in thermoplastic tooling, design and injection molding.

EXPERIENCE:
- Proven abilities in plastic injection troubleshooting, two-color molding, production setups, tool samples and capability studies.

- Skilled in CNC machinery programming, microscopes, CMMs, CIMCAD, CADKEY and Design View; proficient in Excel, Lotus 1-2-3 WordPerfect, DOS, UNIX and Macintosh systems.

- Perform tool studies; trained in metallurgy, steel tooling, jigs/fixtures, production and project management.

EMPLOYMENT: Armin Molding, South Elgin, IL   1/93–Present
Process / Quality Engineer
Supervise and inspect production of medical and commercial injection molded plastic products.
Directly involved in production setups, tooling changes and production troubleshooting.
Supervise up to 12 employees in production and quality control procedures.
* Develop capability studies for sample injection molds.
* Perform quality audits on finished goods.
* Plan and conduct meetings on quality control and individual worker performance.
* Write procedures for production equipment and processes.

APEX/Division of Cooper Industries, Dayton, OH   1990–1991
Cooperative Education Student
Worked extensively with metallurgists and machinists in quality control, inspection and product design.
Controlled surveys in salt bath heat treatment furnaces.
* Produced technical documentation from test data and maintained part gauging calibration for military aircraft universal joints.
* Developed cost-saving tooling improvement methods via state-of-the-art design changes and titanium nitride coatings.

EDUCATION: Ohio University, Athens, OH   Graduated 11/92
B.S. Degree: Industrial Technology
Minor: Business Administration   GPA: 3.1/4.0
* Four-Year Member: Society of Manufacturing Engineers.
* Self-funded 90% of college costs.
* Active in Weight Lifting Club and Habitat for Humanity.

CUTTER SHARP

1132 Cane Garden Circle
Aurora, IL 60504

Residence: 708/555-6144
Cellular Phone: 708/555-8544

MEAT PROCESSING / FOOD INDUSTRY
Willing to Travel or Relocate

PROFILE:

▶ Extensive background in virtually all aspects of meat processing and purveyor operations, specializing in sausage preparation and formula innovation, in retail and manufacturing environments.

▶ Skilled in merchandising, sales, competitor analysis, purchasing, inventory control, advertising/promotions and customer service; experience in facility layouts, equipment and maintenance.

▶ Well-versed in formulas, meat selection and production processes; supervise quality control and adherence to health regulations, including HASB; utilize smokehouses, ovens and steamers efficiently; winner of the national Grand Championship for three different items in 1995.

EMPLOYMENT: CUB Foods, Naperville, IL   5/85–Present
Sausage Maker
In charge of the cooking, display and sale of prepared foods, including smoked ham, chicken, meat loaf and sausage, with responsibility for quality workmanship, formulas and departmental gross margins and revenues.
Directly grind, spice and stuff a variety of sausages; order materials. Handle all counter displays, product demonstrations weekly ads and promotions.

→ Member, American Cured Meat Association.
→ Set up the meat sections for four store openings, in accordance with layouts; developed the merchandising program.
→ Achieved revenues of over $200,000 in 1995, with expectations to exceed the 1996 sales goal.

Jewel Stores, Melrose Park, IL   1/76–10/84
Foreman / Meat Processor, Plant Operations
Supervised 15 employees in a wide range of meat processing and prepared food manufacturing activities, including raw material handling, formulas and packaging, with special attention to health and sanitation regulations. Coordinated daily facility cleanup, setup and maintenance operations. Handled USDA inspections as Journeyman Meat Cutter.

EDUCATION: Triton Community College, River Forest, IL
Course work towards an A.A. degree in mathematics.

Kelly High School, Chicago, IL

HERALD A. THREAT

23762 Bluff Street, Apt. 204
Carol Stream, IL 60188   708/555-1702

MECHANICAL MAINTENANCE / REPAIR

PROFILE:
▶ Extensive background in all aspects of the maintenance/repair of aircraft and vehicles, with responsibility for inspection, problem determination and prompt corrective action in team environments.

▶ Knowledge of parts specifications and applications; well-versed in researching, identifying and pricing parts.

▶ <u>Skilled in a wide range of maintenance processes and equipment:</u>
Tolerance settings utilizing a torque wrench
Corrosion control and aircraft painting
Comprehensive modification of aircraft structures
Balancing of control surfaces and manufacture of control cables
Sheet metal repair and familiar with fiberglass/bonded honeycomb repair
Removal and replacement of skin panels and aircraft fasteners
TA-75/JG-75 tow tractors & NC-8A portable electrical trucks

EMPLOYMENT:
<u>Toyota of Westmont,</u> Westmont, IL   7/95-Present
Parts Specialist
Respond to customer and mechanic requests for automotive parts information promptly and accurately for this dealership with 300 units on the lot and an average of up to 60 units sold monthly; retrieve data for over 4,000 parts from a microfiche system; utilize an online database system to look up pricing information.
Complete and submit customer service forms to assigned mechanics.
→ Contribute to the departmental average monthly sales of $10,000.

<u>Lombard Toyota,</u> Lombard, IL   8/94-7/95
Parts Specialist
Performed the same functions utilizing a TDM/EDI network system for this dealership with 150 units on the lot and sales of 40 units per month.

<u>Sewell Toyota,</u> Odessa, TX   7/93-7/94
Parts Specialist
Served at this dealership with 80 units on the lot and sales of 25 units per month.

MILITARY:
<u>U.S. Navy,</u> San Diego, CA   6/89-6/93
Electrician / Mechanical Equipment Repair, Grade E-3
Maintained and repaired S-3 Squadron air anti-submarine aircraft.
→ Received required support equipment licenses issued by the Command.
→ Inspected aircraft before/after flights as an Airman/Plane Captain, 1989-1990; performed walkarounds with pilots.
→ Promoted to Corrosion Control-9, 1992-1993; detected, removed, treated and restored paint finishes on six S-3B aircraft.

TRAINING:
<u>Numerous schools and courses completed include:</u>
■ 1992, Mathematics/Communications/Airwing Weapons Training (USS Nimitz)
■ 1991, S-3 Connector Repair

EDUCATION:
<u>Odessa High School,</u> Odessa, TX   Graduated 1989
Participated in the work program at Sewell Toyota as a Bodyman's Helper.

DIANA KOVITZ

2214 Roosevelt Road
Hanover Park, IL 60103

630/555-6649

INJECTION MOLDING

PROFILE:

- ▶ Comprehensive experience in job scheduling, work flow management, conflict resolution, team building, motivation and training.
- ▶ Skilled in the operation of a wide variety of injection molding equipment such as Mitsubishi, Cincinnati Milacron, Nissei and Van Dorn Presses; handle communications in a professional manner.
- ▶ Handle multiple aspects of shop operations, including maintenance, tool shop, materials handling and machine processing.

EXPERIENCE:

<u>American Flange Company,</u> Carol Stream, IL 1997-Present
Lead Technician
Effectively manage shift operations including safety and quality assurance.
Assist in training and supervising a staff of six operators in injection molding.

<u>Fellows Manufacturing Co.,</u> Itasca, IL 1983-1997
Cell Leader 1995-1997
Responsible for all aspects of operations for the cell, including scheduling, quality assurance and machine equipment maintenance.
Trained and evaluated a staff of eight machine operators.
Scheduled and organized work through the cell to optimize efficiency and productivity.
- → Ensured quality control through examination of product and training of operators.
- → Assisted other cells in identifying and resolving specific problems.

Shift Lead / Foreman 1988-1995
Directed all shift operations such as assignment of duties, quality control, safety, scheduling and staffing.
Oversaw a team of up to 52 trained workers; hired, evaluated and developed team members and handled personnel issues as needed.
Directed all machine set-ups and arranged for training on specific equipment.
- → Maintained very high safety and quality standards.
- → Effectively communicated with other shift managers and supervisors to update on status of operations.

Process Technician 1987-1988
Set up machines and solved a variety of equipment problems.

Set-up Technician 1985-1987

Material Handler 1983-1985

TRAINING:

Successfully completed a variety of certification and training courses, including <u>Paulson Interactive Training</u>, <u>Nissei America, Inc.</u>, <u>Supervision & Team Building</u> and various in-house programs. **Certified: Injection Molding**; Northern IL. Univ. Bus. & Ind. classes.

SEND T. SPINNER

671 Waterfall Lane
Hanover Park, IL 60103

630/555-3602

ELECTRICAL / MOTOR REPAIR

PROFILE:

▶ Skilled in all aspects of motor repair and maintenance procedures, including worker training and supervision in safety and all shop procedures.

▶ Highly self-motivated and energetic, with a sharp eye for detail and quality; utilize calipers, micrometers, metric and inch measurements.

▶ Fluent in written and spoken Vietnamese.

EXPERIENCE:

Dreisilker Electrical Motors, Glen Ellyn, IL   7/76-10/98
Shop Repair & Maintenance
Responsible for training and supervising up to 4 in all shop procedures, including the complete teardown, repair assembly and test running of electrical motors.
Gained extensive skills with a wide range of equipment, including the troubleshooting and maintenance of:

→ Sleeve and ball-bearing motors up to 5000 h.p.
→ Medium and large: generators, slipring motors, vertical high thrust hollow shaft pump motors.
→ AC and DC motors up to 5000 h.p.
→ Medium and large induction synchronous motors, as well as eddy current clutch motors.

▶ Repair special grinder and hermetic motors, including removing stator and install medium and large vertical motor thrust pumps.
▶ Install and braze rotor bars and connect endrings.
▶ Strip and pull windings from stators; work with gear motors and handle all mechanical work.
▶ Inspect and measure shafts and bearing housings; produce status reports for management.

EDUCATION:

High School Graduate / Equivalent

MILITARY:

U.S. Green Berets, South Vietnam
Lieutenant / Cambodian Army
Repaired and maintained of a wide range of weapons and mechanical systems.

PERSONAL:

Non-smoker, with a strong aptitude for learning electrical and mechanical systems.

WERNER B. HOGAN

234 Dover Drive
Elgin, IL 60120

847/555-4706

PARTS MANAGER / DEALERSHIP OPERATIONS

PROFILE:

▶ Experience in business operations and full sales support, including inventory control, computer system setup and troubleshooting.

▶ Assist in staff hiring, training and supervision in data compilation, report preparation, collections and customer service.

▶ Skilled in various ADP systems as well as Windows, Quicken and MS Works for spreadsheets, word processing and databases.

EMPLOYMENT:

Woodfield Ford, Schaumburg, IL   1988-Present
Assistant Manager, Parts Department
In charge of all parts department activities including hiring, training and supervising six employees in counter operations, parts receiving/stocking and deliveries.
Responsible for all computer system maintenance, updates and tape backups.
Structure prices and assist in collections for past-due invoices.
Utilize ADP parts management and inventory control software; execute all price updates, wholesale incentives and DOES (Direct Order Entry System).
Calculate profit margins and determine costs.
Train all personnel in processing claims, shortages, damaged goods, back orders, overages and shortages.
* Personally established all major department computer procedures.
* Certified Ford Parts Specialist.

Heritage Lincoln Mercury, Elgin, IL   1986-1988
Parts Manager
Effectively trained and supervised two employees in data entry, report generation and all department procedures.
* Winner of Ford's Silver Medallion Award (1st year) and the Bronze Medallion (2nd year).

Packey Webb Ford, Wheaton, IL   1984-1986
Parts Counter
Performed direct customer service and updated/maintained accurate parts inventories.
Worked closely with managers to process paperwork.
* Implemented Ford's new DCS computer system.

EDUCATION:

Elgin Community College: Basic Computer Skills
Control Data Company: Insight Training
Ford Motor Company: DCS/UCS Computer Training

PERSONAL:

Strong aptitude for computers and electronics; skilled in soldering and assembly.

JOHN VAN GOGH

2310 W. St. Charles Road #3
Villa Park, IL 60181

708/555-7524

PROFESSIONAL PAINTER

EXPERIENCE:
- Proven abilities in interior and exterior painting, including full responsibility for surface preparation and paint selection; Certified, Journeyman Painter.

- Experience with all types of wall covering, enamel/latex paints, color mixing and coding.

- Skilled in painting walls, floors, ceilings, doors, boiler rooms and exterior surfaces including signs.

EMPLOYMENT:
Oakbrook Terrace Tower, Oakbrook Terrace, IL   10/87-4/99
Painter
Responsible for interior and exterior painting using all skills listed above.
Performed accurate cost and time estimating for all jobs.
Ordered paints and supplies from vendors in a cost-effective manner.
Painted tenant offices, storage locations and boiler and utility rooms.
* Provided prompt, courteous service for all tenants and staff.

C.E.F. Industries, Addison, IL   2/80-2/86
Department Supervisor
Trained and supervised two employees in the production of flexible shafts.
Inspected all work and ensured excellent product quality.
* Scheduled production and improved procedures, resulting in greater efficiency and productivity.
* Promoted to this position from Factory Worker.

Crafts Unlimited, Elk Grove Village, IL   6/74-12/79
Working Supervisor
Responsible for paint/color mixing for painting and finishing of industrial models, patterns and prototypes to customer specifications.

EDUCATION:
Training, Inc., Lombard, IL   3/86-6/86
Trained in accounting, business math, records management, touch calculator, general office skills and human relations.

Industrial Management Institute, Westchester, IL   12/80-5/82
Certificates in Supervision, Industrial Management and Psychology.

Northern Illinois Painter's Apprentice School, Batavia, IL
Certificate   1990

Glenbard North High School, Carol Stream, IL   Graduated 1974

147

ALBERT M. LENS

2270 Madrid Court
Hanover Park, IL 60103   lensman@aol.com   630/555-0871

PHOTOGRAPHY / FILM

PROFILE:	▸ Skilled in creative photography, film and video production from concept to final editing, including promotional and art shots in color and B&W, with 35 mm, medium and large format cameras.
	▸ Experience with Hasselblad and Mamiya (medium format) cameras and 4"x 5" view cameras; handle creative developing and darkroom procedures; experience in PhotoShop 4.0 and Avid.
	▸ Featured in various galleries and publications, including **Photographer's Forum Magazine's** hard-bound edition, *The Best of College Photography, 1998.*
	▸ Fluent in Spanish; traveled extensively throughout Europe, 7/98-9/98.

PHOTO EXHIBITS:

Group Exhibitions:

New Works Gallery, Chicago, IL   5/98 and 12/97

University of Illinois, Champaign, IL   10/97

FILM & VIDEO WORKS:

Personally wrote, produced and directed:
- Faith: (Experimental, 1996) Examination of elements in a church, 3.5 minutes.
- Maestro de Guitarra: (Documentary, 1997) Guitar performances and interviews, 14.5 minutes.

INTERNSHIPS:

Paul Elledge Studio, Chicago, IL   Summer, 1997
Kevin Banna and Frederic Stein Studios, Chicago, IL   Summer, 1996

EDUCATION:

University of Illinois at Chicago, Chicago, IL   Graduated 5/98
Bachelor of Fine Arts Degree
Major: Photography, Film and Electronic Media.
- Dean's List, 5 semesters.   • Graduated with Honors.
- Golden Key National Honors Society and Phi Kappa Phi National Honors Society.

W.R. Harper College, Palatine, IL   Graduated 12/95
Associate of Arts Degree

EMPLOYMENT:

Illinois Shotokan Karate Clubs, Palatine, IL   1/92-Present
Club Photographer / Instructor
Document and instruct students of all ages, ranked up to black belt.

U.S. Marines: Of a platoon of 86, one of only 5 recruits to graduate with Meritorious Promotion. Stationed in Kuwait and Saudi Arabia during Desert Shield and Desert Storm.

MEMBERSHIP:

Member: American Society of Media Photographers.

DIANE BONES

224N30 Kenwood Road
West Chicago, IL 60185   630/555-1607

PHYSICAL THERAPIST ASSISTANT

PROFILE:

- Highly skilled in all aspects of physical therapy, including file updating, accurate documentation, physician liaison and extensive patient contact.

- Certified as a **Physical Therapist Assistant** in the State of Illinois; successfully completed clinicals in physical therapy in outpatient, acute care, nursing home and work environments at various Chicagoland healthcare institutions.

- Consistently recognized by management and patients for superior talents in troubleshooting and problem resolution in high-pressure situations.

EMPLOYMENT: Alexian Brothers Medical Center, Elk Grove Village, IL   1992-Present
Physical Therapist Assistant II
Responsible for patient care, treatment plans, chart updating, weekly summary reports and communications with nurses and physicians.
Familiar with Geriatric, Orthopedics, Sports Medicine and Manual Therapy.
Gained experience in training and prevention programs.

- → One of the few PTAs trained in Myofascial Release.
- → Work part-time with pediatric clients at Rosewood Therapy Challenge in Libertyville, IL from 1998-Present.
- → Serve as a Clinical Instructor for PTA students.
- → Work closely with volunteer aides in daily tasks.
- → Promoted to this position from PTA I because of excellent work performance.

EDUCATION: Oakton Community College, Des Plaines, IL   1992
A.A.S. Degree in Physical Therapy

Elgin Community College, Elgin, IL   1992
A.S. Degree in General Studies

**ADDITIONAL
TRAINING:**

- → Myofascial Release, Muscle Energy to Lumbar, Spine & Pelvis, Strain/ Counterstrain, Integrative Therapy for Low Back and Lower Quadrant, Building & Rebuilding the Complete Athlete and Preferred Roles of the PTA.

DENNIS E. CLOUD

2291 Ashley Drive
Granger, IN 46530

219/555-4841

OBJECTIVE: **Pilot:** A position utilizing skills as Flight Crew member.

EXPERIENCE:
- Proven abilities as pilot, first officer and mechanic, including full flight management responsibilities.

- Flight Time: PIC 3000, SIC 4400, MEL 6300, SEL 1100, CFI 363.

- Total Flight Time: 7500; SIC Turbo Prop 4200, SIC Turbo Jet 182, Instrument 800, Cross Country 6500, Night 1400.

- Certificates: ATP MEL/SEL; CFI SEL FEW/Passed; A&P certificate.

EMPLOYMENT:

Atlantic Coast Airlines, Washington/Dulles Airport, Herdon, VA
Captain: DHC-8, BAe J-4100   9/93-Present

Air Wisconsin, Inc., Outgamie Airport, Appleton, WI
First Officer   5/89-9/93
Responsible for numerous flights in the F-27 Fokker, SD3-60 and BAe ATP.

Northwest Airlines, Inc., Hartsfield Intnl. Airport, Atlanta, GA
A&P Mechanic   7/88-5/89
Handled troubleshooting and maintenance of C-CKs, DC-9s and B-727s.

Aerospec, Inc., Falcon Field, Peachtree City, GA
Pilot / A&P Mechanic   3/88-7/88

Eastern Metro Express, Hartsfield International Airport, Atlanta, GA
First Officer - Jetstream 31   5/87-3/88
Part 135 - 121 Regional Carrier.

Eastern Airlines, Inc., Hartsfield, International Airport, Atlanta, GA
A&P Mechanic   10/79-5/87
Responsible for phase check: B-727, B-757, DC-9, A-300, L-1011, D-Check, B-727, DC-9, L-1011 and the A-300.

EDUCATION:

Embry-Riddle Aeronautical University, Daytona Beach, FL   1974-1976
Studies in Aeronautical Science and Airport Management.

Spartan School of Aeronautics, Tulsa, OK   1972-1973
Airframe and Power Plant License

MILITARY:

U.S. Army, **Flight Engineer on Turbine Powered Aircraft**   11/69-6/72
Completed U.S. Army Turbine/Airframe Repair Training.
Completed more than 2000 hours of flight time.

DAVID E. WINGTIP

2267 Thomas Drive
East Troy, WI 53120

414/555-4141
708/555-9368

OBJECTIVE: **CORPORATE PILOT**

FLIGHT RATINGS:

Airline Transport Pilot: MEL
A.T.P. Type Rating in BE-1900, BE-300
Commercial Pilot: SEL; Instrument
Flight Instructor: Airplane SEL/MEL; Instrument

First Class Medical - No Restrictions
No Accidents or Violations

FLIGHT TIME:

TOTAL TIME:	3801
Multi-Engine:	2981
Total P.I.C.:	1500
Total S.I.C.:	2108
Multi-Engine P.I.C.:	807
Turbine:	2198
Instructor Pilot:	1240
Instrument:	337

EDUCATION:

B.S. Degree in Aeronautical Science (December 1987)
Embry-Riddle Aeronautical University, Daytona Beach, FL
National Dean's List 1985-1987
GPA: 3.39/4.00

EXPERIENCE:

5/91-4/93
AIR WISCONSIN, INC., Appleton, WI
First Officer, deHavilland Dash 8, Part 121 Scheduled Airline

7/90-1/91
BAR HARBOR AIRWAYS, Miami, FL
Captain, Beach 1900, Part 135 Scheduled Airline

5/89-6/90
ATLANTIC SOUTHEAST AIRLINES, Atlanta, GA
First Officer, Embraer 120 Brasilia, Part 135 Scheduled Airline

8/88-5/89
AIRLINE TRANSPORT PROFESSIONALS, Atlanta, GA
Flight Instructor, Light Twin Engine

ROCCO PODGORNIAK

2272 First Avenue
Bartlett, IL 60103   630/555-1215

PLANT MANAGEMENT / PRODUCT DEVELOPMENT

PROFILE:

▸ Comprehensive experience in all aspects of plant operations including expediting, purchasing, equipment maintenance and inventory control.

▸ Skilled in product design, with a proven ability to conceptualize, draft and fabricate products.

▸ Proficient in a wide range of technical skills including electrical, pipe fitting, welding (arc, mig, tig, gas) hydraulics, pneumatics, steel fabrication, forklift operations and material handling.

EXPERIENCE:

Flight Ways Corporation, Batavia, IL   1997-1999
General Manager / Senior Engineer
Responsible for all aspects of product design including drawings, prototyping and production.
Worked with other team members to fully develop concepts from concept stage to completion.
→ Calculated and reduced material costs through vendor negotiations.

Cutting Edge, Batavia, IL   1994-1997
Manager
Handled employee management and training, job assignment and supervision of plant operations for this company employed in rebuilding used shredding equipment.

Shredd Pax Corporation, Wood Dale, IL   1992-1994
Shop Manager
Responsible for all daily operations of the welding and assembly departments including staff supervision and work flow organization.
Planned and implemented production improvements in the fabrication department.

Sunrise Welding, Bartlett, IL   1987-1992
General Manager / Owner
Directed all day-to-day activities including business development, customer relations, personnel and hands-on production.
Performed welding activities using various materials and appropriate techniques.

EDUCATION:

Southeast Illinois College   1987-1990
→ Completed various industry training courses.

EDWARD J. PLANTMAN

22751 Sunnyside Road
Roselle, IL 60172   630/555-5055

OBJECTIVE: **OPERATIONS / PLANT MANAGEMENT**
Industrial Manufacturing & Distribution

PROFILE:
- ▶ Extensive background in virtually all warehouse service and industrial manufacturing operations, with hands-on production supervisory responsibilities in customer-driven, ISO 9002 certified, team environments.
- ▶ Skilled in troubleshooting and problem resolution; train and supervise machine operators in quality, adherence to work order specifications and equipment maintenance on Chicago 60", 48" Monarch stamco and 12"-18" slitters, Dahlstrom 48" cut-to-length machines and 18"-20" edgers; **Certified Internal Quality Auditor.**

EMPLOYMENT: Precision Steel Warehouse, Franklin Park, IL   1979-Present
A privately held service steel warehouse set up to cut metals for job shops; part of Precision Steel with two other branches in North Carolina and Illinois.
Slitting Supervisor   6/92-Present
Responsible for all slitting operations, including setups/teardowns, basic equipment maintenance, work order completion and adherence to quality control standards.
Train and supervise 26 employees on four 12" to 60" slitters to cut coils to specified widths.
Program gauges on the digital Chicago slitter; check and adjust tolerance limits.
Inspect coils for defects before production startup.
Order warehouse supplies and submit orders for equipment/tools such as grinding slitting knives, lumber and packaging paper products.
Hold monthly safety meetings to review accident rates and prevention measures; C.P.R. and Basic First Aid certified.
- → Key customers include Allen Bradley, Square D, Eaton and Acco International.
- → Part of ISO 9002 certification team; drafted job descriptions.
- → Utilize a PC system to process staff bonuses based on piecework per hour.
- → Contributed to a 30% reduction in rejections over the prior four years.

Cut-length Supervisor   6/88-6/92
Supervised up to 17 people on seven machines to cut/edge steel coils.
Produced a master production staffing schedule, including overtime and vacations.
- → Managed the UPS Department.
- → Promoted to this position from **Operator,** 4/82-8/88; hired as a **Coil Handler, Packaging,** 4/79-4/82.

RECOGNITION: Medinah Park District, Award for Outstanding Contributions to the Park and Recreation movement in Illinois, from the Suburban Park and Recreation Association.

TRAINING: MIMA Management Institute courses in Supervision, Key Link to Productivity I & II, Advanced Supervisory Techniques I & II, Communication in the Real World, Training the Employee on the Job and Principles and Practices of Management I & II.

EDUCATION: Riverdale High School, Muscoda, WI

Mitch Vice

2253 South Victoria Lane
Streamwood, IL 60107

630/555-4825

POLICE OFFICER

PROFILE:

▶ Extensive training in police procedures including patrol duty, traffic stops, warrants, search procedures and apprehensions.

▶ Trained in a criminal justice theory and effective written and oral communications for law enforcement.

▶ Familiar with computer systems including Windows 98 and various programs for data entry and retrieval.

EDUCATION:

College of DuPage, Glen Ellyn, IL   Present
Criminal Justice Program
Currently attending courses in Police Operations and Procedures.

* Courses include training in all daily police procedures, including those listed above.
* Enrolled to attend courses in Criminal Justice and Composition in the Winter semester.

EMPLOYMENT:

Batesville Casket Company, Glendale Heights, IL   12/93-Present
Driver
Responsible for extensive driving and prompt deliveries to businesses in the Northwest suburbs.
Developed a strong knowledge of streets and highways.
Communicate with customers to ensure accurate shipments.

* Maintained an excellent driving record.

Osman Construction Company, Arlington Heights, IL 1988-1991, 1992-1993
Laborer
Involved in a wide range of commercial construction projects.

Lisle Electric, Sycamore, IL   1991-1992
Apprentice Electrician
Performed wiring of electrical systems for new homes.

JOHN J. ROLLER

2205 W. Golden Drive
Glendale Heights, IL 60139

708/555-5844

PRESS MAINTENANCE / MANAGEMENT

EXPERIENCE:
- Skilled in pressroom operations including full responsibility for teardowns, rebuilds and maintenance.

- Comprehensive experience with various web presses: roll to fold, roll to roll and roll to sheet.

- Utilize dry and wet offset presses and Hamilton, Ashton and Harris equipment, as well as collators and PCMs.

- Effectively hire, train and supervise workers in all aspects of press setup, repair and hazardous waste handling and disposal.

EMPLOYMENT: Distributor Stock Forms, Addison, IL   12/86-Present
Maintenance Manager
Responsible for training and supervising three employees in the troubleshooting, repair and maintenance of printing presses and equipment at three locations.
Perform cost-effective purchasing of parts, maintenance supplies and material handling equipment.

* Oversee all aspects of hazardous waste disposal and building and press preventive maintenance.
* Work directly with building and fire inspectors with a strong knowledge of building and fire safety codes and standards.

CST Group, Wheeling, IL   4/79-12/86
Pressman / Maintenance
Effectively operated and maintained Hamilton Presses, Collators and PCMs.
Handled all aspects of troubleshooting, repair and maintenance.
Repaired and operated material handling equipment.

* Supervised preventive maintenance procedures for the entire building.

EDUCATION: High School Graduate

Hamilton School
Completed special training in press systems.

PERSONAL: High aptitude for electrical and mechanical system troubleshooting.
Self-motivated, energetic and detail-minded.
Mature, team player and a strong motivator.

NELSON A. COLOR

2234 South Justine Street
Chicago, IL 60620

312/555-4749

PRE-PRESS OPERATIONS

PROFILE:

- ▶ Experience in virtually all aspects of pre-press operations in team environments; specializing in disk to output with strict attention to quality control.
- ▶ Skilled in camera-ready setup, file conversions, proofing, imaging, trapping, sizing and transferring files to output devices.
- ▶ <u>Proficient in numerous systems and equipment:</u>
  Scitex PS/2, Iris 3024, Dolev, AGFA/Selectset 5000 and Eray image setters; Scitex imager; Cromalin proofing; Hell Chromograph CP3900 scanner; and Fuji ScanArt scanner; familiar with Macintosh, QuarkXpress, PhotoShop and Adobe Illustrator.

EMPLOYMENT:

<u>Precision Color Imaging,</u> Addison, IL   1991-Present
Macintosh Operator, 2nd Shift
Perform pre-press responsibilities for this subsidiary of Fenton Press, specializing in commercial advertising including 1/2/4-color ads, newsletters and publications; clients include Women's Health Magazine, Celestine Journal and Cahners.
→ Occasionally work on DuPont waterproofs and a Crossfield scanner.

<u>JohnsByrne Company,</u> Niles, IL   1994-1996
Macintosh Operator, 2nd Shift
Reformatted images from customer files for output to film according to job ticket specifications for this printer specializing in baseball cards.
Trained in scanning files, color correction and page assembly.
Adjusted line screens, and D'Max and excurve images.
Sent files to the PS/2 and Dolev 400 image setters for output with trapping.
Checked film detail against customer boards or laser copy; submitted film for proofing.
Checked Dylux, Kodak signature and Cromalin proofs for discrepancies.
Occasionally shot camera-ready copy.
Retrieved, edited and reran archived files from DAT tapes.

<u>Noral Color,</u> Chicago, IL   1989-1994
Plotter Specialist / Proofer
Output film from Scitex image setters; prepare and resize pickups.
Produced matchprint, DuPont waterproof, Cromalin and Dylux proofs.
Shot camera-ready art and copy; maintained film and proofing processors.

<u>Color Image,</u> Long Beach, CA   1987-1989
Camera Man / Black & White Scanner Operator
Sized B&W prints and 4-color transparencies; output film from Hell image setters.
Utilized the Fuju scanner to scan B&W prints to half-tones.
Contacted and proofed film for stripping; produced proofs of various types.

EDUCATION:

<u>William Rainey Harper Community College,</u> Palatine, IL   4/95
Coursework in Advanced Quark on a Macintosh system.

<u>Chicago Graphic Arts Project,</u> Chicago, IL   6/81-9/81
Diploma in Offset Lithography

CINDY BOX

226 Linden Drive
Carol Stream, IL 60188

708/555-0803

PRINTING / PRESS OPERATIONS

PROFILE:

▶ Extensive background in virtually all aspects of printing, with responsibility for press configurations, setups and teardowns.

▶ Skilled in color matching, fusing, collating, trimming and packing functions; pre-set machines strictly to job order specifications.

▶ Experience with 2-color web presses, including the Didde Glaser roll-to-sheet web and collator machines, and ARC fusing machines; enter job data into the computer tracking/pricing database system.

EMPLOYMENT: Avery-Dennison, Inc., Rolling Meadows, IL   10/87-Present
Rotate among various areas of press operations, utilizing Didde Glaser and ARC equipment, to produce a wide range of office paper products.

Web Press Operator
Set up and operate the web press after verifying the paper weight, color and size, and the plates for style, size of paper, type and tab cut extension.
Check job order for punching holes, reinforcement, trimming and sheet cutting.
Inspect final work for discrepancies; send to fusing for further processing.
Handle routine machine maintenance and repair.

Fusing Machine Operator
Utilize an ARC fusing machine to set back feeder to specifications for ribbon size, tab size and extension, and mylar ribbons and RIP.
Inspect job after collating and before start of fusing; proof titles, position tabs and select mylars.

Collator
Inspect final job for defects including smudges, spelling/typographical errors, incorrect color of paper and wrong tab sizes/extensions.
Collate materials into job sets; pack, seal and label boxes and place job sets into cases for shipping.

Homemaker   1980-1987
Managed family matters and maintained the home on relocating to the U.S.

EDUCATION: ITT Institute, Bhanditina, India   Graduated 1975
Diploma / Certificate in Teaching

Government College, Punjab, India   Graduated 1972
Bachelor of Arts degree in Economics / Political Science
Minor: English

KEN DOLOTS

8989 Andrene Lane
Itasca, IL 60143   708/555-0290

OBJECTIVE: *PRODUCTION OPERATIONS / ASSEMBLY*

EXPERIENCE:

- More than nine years in production operations, including responsibility for line setup, worker training and quality assurance.

- Work directly with engineers and managers in procedure planning, parts ordering, status reporting and efficiency.

- Skilled in computer system use for inventory tracking and bills of material.

- Hire, train and supervise staff in equipment use and maintenance, QA and plant safety.

EMPLOYMENT: Sunstar Laboratories, Inc., Bensenville, IL   1982-Present
Production Supervisor
Responsible for setup and management of various liquid fill and assembly lines for the packaging of fragrances, hand/body lotions, liquid/bar soaps, deodorants and anti-perspirants.
Brand names include Jovan, Aspen, Adidas and Yardley.
Compile daily production reports and utilize Tandem and Sequel software; verify components and bills of material for inventory control and efficient, on-time production.
Work with department engineers for new item changes and updates.

- Efficiency at this plant is up 20% plantwide, 1996-present.
- Department rejects have dropped at a record rate, 1997-present.
- Train, supervise and conduct performance reviews for up to 50 employees utilizing MRM vacuum fillers, U.S. Bottler vacuum fillers, J&G fillers, Horix fillers, Elgin Sextet, Cavella Fillers, National Fill-A-Matic Fillers, Resina Cappers, Pro+ spin cappers, J.G. Crimpers and labelers by Avery, Precision, Patton and New Jersey.
- Maintain excellent productivity rates and product quality standards.
- Perform quality assurance checks on a regular basis.

EDUCATION: Elmhurst College, Elmhurst, IL
B.S. Degree - Business Major   Graduated 1981

College of DuPage, Glen Ellyn, IL   1977-1979
Completed several business and general courses.

Alan A. Pipeline

2344 Springvalley Lane
Streamwood, IL 60107

630/555-7562

PUBLIC WORKS

PROFILE:
- ▶ Comprehensive experience in all aspects of public works and building maintenance, including snow/ice control, water meter service/installation, street cleaning and sewerage.

- ▶ Skilled a variety of functions such as forklift repair, arc welding, electrical, plumbing, snow removal, fire hydrant repair, valves and service lines.

- ▶ Operate end loaders, street sweepers, sewer flushers, back hoe, dump trucks and other small equipment. CDL trained and licensed, including tankers.

EXPERIENCE: Village of Itasca   June 1989 - May 1999
Public Works
Handled all aspects of providing public works services, including staffing, organizing work, performing all functions, budgeting and supervision.
Installed, repaired and read water meters.
Repaired water main breaks; installed and repaired fire hydrants and water main valves. Handled snow removal and street cleaning.
Operated various equipment/machinery in performing duties, including sewer flusher, end loaders, 2 1/2 ton dump trucks, back hoe and black top roller.
- → Directed the activities of five departments; served as Superintendent.
- → Completed a range of training programs.

F.W. Woolworth Co.   June 1979-May 1989
Building Maintenance
Performed a wide range of maintenance work such as electrical, plumbing and equipment repair.
Maintained and repaired a completely automated conveyor system, low pressure boilers and forklift trucks.
Programmed route sorters. Handled snow removal.

TRAINING: Completed a variety of applicable seminars and training including:

Business Management	Safety in the Workplace
Confined Space Entry	Snow and Ice Control
Blood Borne Pathogens	First Aid and CPR
Trench Safety	Disaster Control and Response
Defensive Driving	Equipment Repair and
Maintenance	
Water Meter Touch and Phone Read	

EDUCATION: Downers Grove Community High School
Downers Grove, IL (GED)

159

GOTTA B. PERFECT

2356 Marcie Court, #9
Addison, IL 60101   708/555-3224

OBJECTIVE: *QUALITY CONTROL INSPECTOR*
A position utilizing proven skills in electrical and mechanical applications.

EXPERIENCE:
- Familiar with the use of precision measuring instruments.

- More than six years in drafting and CAD operations, including responsibility for a wide range of product and system designs.

- Proficient in AUTOCAD and Microstation/Intergraph.

- Skilled in blueprint and schematic reading, interpretation and development.

- Work directly with engineers and technical staff in configurations and upgrades; solid background in trigonometry, geometry and algebra.

EMPLOYMENT: Sterling Technical Consulting, Inc., Westchester, IL   1/91-12/93
CAD Designer
Responsible for updating and computerization of manually drafted mechanical drawings using AUTOCAD versions 10 and 11.
Involved in re-draw work of blueprints for Commonwealth Edison residential and commercial power configurations.

Circuit Systems, Inc., Elk Grove Village, IL   3/89-1/91
Quality Control Inspector
Checked quality of printed circuit boards utilizing a micrometer, vernier and diameter gauge.

Elicon Company, V.V. Nagar, India   9/86-2/89
Draftsman
Worked directly with engineers and updated product sketches to strict quality control standards.
Utilized precision measurement equipment for inspections of final products.
* Currently employed at Prudential Insurance Co. as a <u>Sales Representative.</u>

EDUCATION: **B.S. Degree Equivalent: Mechanical Engineering**   1987
S.P. University, V.V. Nagar, India

Certificate: Microstation/Intergraph   1990
College of DuPage, Glen Ellyn, IL

Certificate: Mechanical Drafting and Design   1989-1991
College of DuPage, Glen Ellyn, IL

Richard M. Checkout

2258 Beech Court
Carol Stream, IL 60188   630/555-1371

OBJECTIVE: ***An opportunity to utilize my experience and skills in quality control.***

PROFILE:
- ▶ Comprehensive experience in a wide range of business operations including quality assurance/control, staff scheduling, inventory control, freight forwarding, shipping and receiving.

EXPERIENCE: Mechanical Electrical Automation, Elk Grove Village, IL   1/92-Present
Quality Control Manager
Responsible for ensuring that all machined parts meet or exceed production standards.
Accurately read blueprints to determine part specifications.
Inspect parts for accuracy and approve for release to final assembly or reject.
Perform data entry.
Receive and process incoming materials.

Celadon Jacky Maeder, Bensenville, IL   2/90-12/91
Operations
Handled the shipping and receiving of product for this air and ocean freight forwarder.
Performed cost analysis of international shipments and maintained files.

John's Garage Restaurant and Lucky's Diner, Schaumburg, IL   2/83-1/90
Served in various positions including Restaurant Manager, Bar Manager and Bartender for both of these high-volume restaurants under one ownership.
Performed all aspects of inventory control, accounts payable/receivable, pricing, ordering, cash management, staff scheduling, training and customer service.

EDUCATION: College of DuPage and Harper College
- → Successfully completed several computer and business related courses, such as Windows 3.1, as well as the core English requirements.

Elk Grove High School, Elk Grove Village, IL   **Graduate**

TRAINING: Completed training in Metalworking Skills I and Measuring for Quality Control.

INTERESTS: Actively involved in sports, reading and gardening.

LYNDA V. MICROPHONE

2205 Washington Street Cellular: 708/555-5753
Oak Park, IL 60302   Home Phone: 708/555-8077

OBJECTIVE: *INTERNSHIP: RADIO BROADCASTING*
A position where proven communication and technical skills would be utilized.

PROFILE:
- Comprehensive experience in program production, including interviewing, mixing, editing, and final presentation.

- Background in weather and traffic reporting; coordinate talent and create introductions, sound bites, PSAs, and professional formats.

- Hands-on experience as traffic/news reporter and talk show host for numerous programs.

EXPERIENCE: <u>TCI of Illinois, Inc.</u>, Mt. Prospect, IL   1993-Present
Community Public Access TV Producer / Playback Operator
Responsible for all aspects of development for local programs, including story origination, writing, interviews, camera operation, floor direction, sound setup, and final editing.
Coordinate schedules; operate a variety of cameras, sound boards, and editors.
Manage programs from concept to completion; subjects include local artists, authors, and community services.

* Test marketed TCI's Intelligent Television project for audience control of pay-per-view movies and commercial programs.
* Completed numerous TCI training programs in broadcasting and production.

<u>Walden Apartments</u>, Schaumburg, IL   1989-1993
Marketing Director / Leasing Consultant
Manage all aspects of leasing for 619 residential units, including marketing, promotions, and sales presentations.
Handle public relations and written/oral communications in a professional manner.
Coordinate special events and create advertisements.
Assist in training and supervising three employees in creative sales, resident retention/renewal, and special promotions.
* Earned national award for Top Sales and Customer Support.

<u>Draper & Kramer, Inc.</u>, Chicago, IL   1987-1989
Leasing Consultant

EDUCATION: **B.A. Degree: Mass Communications**   Graduated 1987
<u>Rust College</u>, Holly Springs, MS
* Employed as **Announcer / DJ** on a local radio station.
* Earned various awards for producing and hosting a variety of talk show programs and weather, traffic, and news reports.

CARI A. STEELBAG

7736 Cypress Drive
Streamwood, IL 60107   630/555-0916

OBJECTIVE: *RAMP SERVICE / AIRLINE INDUSTRY*
A position where problem-solving and team skills will be of value.

PROFILE:

- Hands-on experience in construction, warehouse and receiving/ shipping functions; proven ability to meet to organize crews, prioritize tasks, meet deadlines and adhere to quality for customer satisfaction.
- Numerous classes attended toward a private pilot license; completed 57/60 flight hours; maintain current in industry trends at EAA/FAA forums and conventions; member: Experimental Aircraft Association (EAA) since 1991.

EMPLOYMENT: <u>Lakeview Lumber Construction,</u> Lake Barrington, IL   10/95-Present
Apprentice Carpenter
Remodel kitchens, bathrooms and basements, including siding/roofing installation and room additions, for multiple and single-family residential construction projects.

<u>JWK Painting,</u> Algonquin, IL   7/95-10/95
Painter
Contracted to paint interior/exterior surfaces of commercial and residential properties.

<u>Classic Contract Cleaning Company,</u> Rolling Meadows, IL   12/94-6/95
Crew Supervisor
Organized, scheduled and supervised crews at multiple locations in cleaning commercial properties, including inventory tracking and equipment maintenance.
→ Responded to customer inquiries and resolved complaints.

<u>Artlow Systems,</u> Addison, IL   11/91-2/92
Laborer   and 6/89-8/89
Performed structural jobs, including paint/sealant removal, joint restoration, mud jacking and floor system seeding.

Other positions include: 1988-1994
Part-time Loader, Overnight Transportation Company; **Stocker,** F&M Distributors
Loader, Roadway Packaging Systems; **Sales Associate, Part-time,** Sportmart, Inc.

MILITARY SERVICE: <u>U.S. Army,</u> Ft. Leonard Wood, MO/Ft. Lewis, WA   1985-1988
Bco. 864th Engineer Bn / Motortransport Operator / Carpenter
Certifications: Bus driver, 44 passengers; vehicle inspection; 64C Motortransport; Army physical readiness test.

EDUCATION: <u>William Rainey Harper College,</u> Palatine, IL   Graduated 1994
<u>Streamwood High School,</u> Streamwood, IL   Graduated 1985

JERRY D. RAIL

220 Cedar Street, Apt. 1A
Glendale Heights, IL 60139

Residence: 630/555-8121
Cellular Phone: 312/555-8099

OBJECTIVE: ***YARDMASTER / RAILROAD OPERATIONS***
A position where communication, organizational, problem-solving and technical skills would be utilized.

PROFILE:
- ▶ Experience in all aspects of field and office operations; plan, organize and conduct training sessions in on-track safety, track buckling, high-rail operations and maintenance of way; assist in safety training examinations.
- ▶ Utilize WordPerfect and Lotus Notes for Windows; authorized to retrieve, track and update a wide range of confidential information; Illinois Commercial Drivers License (CDL); current Brotherhood of Maintenance of Way member.

EMPLOYMENT: <u>Union Pacific Railroad,</u> HQ, Omaha, NE   1989-Present
(formerly Chicago & Northwestern Railroad)

Machine Operator / Special Projects   1/96-Present
Implement a wide range of special projects for this thru-freight and way-freight railroad company in its Illinois/Wisconsin territory, in full compliance with operating rules, state/local regulations and interstate laws.
Key Projects
- → *Track Maintenance and Repair:* organize, schedule and coordinate contractors in a building demolition project and asbestos abatement, including contractor selection.
- → *Field Office Liaison:* coordinate information between corporate and branch offices.
- → *Vehicle Licensing:* review licensing notices and renew/request licenses as needed; recommend vehicular retirement.
- → *Territory Mapping:* prepare charts detailing tracks for use by such staff as inspectors, managers, conductors and locomotive engineers.
- → *Safety Training Classes:* work with Safety Coordinator to administer rules examinations, including participant registration, class scheduling, classroom arrangements and examination grading/evaluation; plan and conduct training in specific topics such as on-track safety.
- → *Safety Captain:* update employees on general orders issued by the Safety Engineering Department; inspect vehicles, observe the work of gangs, check for personal protection equipment and advise on techniques, procedures and policies.

Foreman   1/92-1/96
Managed crews on rotational assignments:
- → **Surfacing Gang.** Organized and supervised machine operators in track surfacing and alignment. Processed timesheets, monitored schedules and controlled crew performance.
- → **Section Gang.** Supervised four machine operators/laborers in general track maintenance, including rail/tie inspection, broken rail repair, installation of ties and crossings reparation.

Machine Operator, Surfacing Gang   8/91-1/92

EDUCATION: <u>Sterling High School,</u> Sterling, IL
Completed the building trades program at Pike Vocational Training Center.

VENICE RAFT

7875 Gross Point Road
Evanston, IL 60201

708/555-4656

REAL ESTATE APPRAISER

PROFILE:

▸ Trained in full property assessment including measuring, picture-taking and analysis of comparable properties; compile and present final reports.

▸ Extensive knowledge of layouts, building materials and codes with experience in the construction industry; handle customer service, negotiations and communications in a professional manner.

▸ Licensed Real Estate Appraiser from the Appraisal Institute, 1995; Licensed Real Estate Sales Representative since 1978; willing to travel.

EDUCATION:

The Appraisal Institute, Chicago, IL   Licensed 4/95
Licensed Real Estate Appraiser
Courses included training in all aspects of residential real estate appraisal, from 1 to 4 units.

Real Estate Sales License Holder   Since 1978
Attended additional training every two years to present.

Northern Illinois University, DeKalb, IL
B.S. Degree: Accounting   Overall GPA: 3.3/4.0

EMPLOYMENT:

Sharp Garage Company, Chicago, IL   1983–Present
Manager
Responsible for all account prospecting, customer service and project management for this builder of custom garages.
Perform marketing and advertising, sales presentations, purchasing and accounting functions.
Supervise sales and office support, as well as independent contractors.
Negotiate contracts and determine/meet customer's specific needs for garages, room additions and remodeling work, including designs and materials.
→ Developed sales from zero to $1.5 million annually through extensive travel and strong self-motivation.

Danley Lumber Company, Westchester, IL   1978-1983
Sale Representative
Worked closely with all types of customers to interpret their needs and design/build custom garages.
→ Ranked #1 in sales of 25 representatives.
→ Developed an extensive referral business by carefully listening to the customer and providing prompt, quality service.

Bernstein & Banks, Ltd. and J.K. Lasser & Co., Chicago, IL   1972-1978
Staff Accountant
Conducted audits and general accounting for numerous companies.

Diana M. Service

43138 Wasdale Avenue
Elk Grove Village, IL 60007

847/555-1569

Objective: ***RESERVATIONS - A customer-focused position in the airline industry such as Flight Attendant or Reservations Professional.***

PROFILE:
- Comprehensive experience in professional customer service; proven ability to identify and meet client needs and expectations.
- Completely fluent (verbal and written) in Spanish and English. Proficient in many major PC applications, including Excel, MS Word, Act and Windows, as well as data entry on customized software.

EXPERIENCE:

Sloan Valve Company, Franklin Park, IL   1994-1999
Assistant to the Manager   1996-1999
Promoted to this position to perform various customer service and administrative functions, including writing correspondence and file/documentation maintenance.
Met client requests for information such as marketing materials and product specifications.
- Developed an Excel spreadsheet to track and calculate monthly sales commissions.

Customer Service / Data Entry   1994-1996
Responsible for entering correspondence in MS Word, creating invoices, maintaining accurate files and handling incoming phone calls.
Provided product information to customers and entered sales orders into customized software package.

USA One National Credit Union, Bensenville, IL   1994
Assistant Branch Supervisor
Responsible for supervising the daily operations of this facility, including handled cash transactions and customer service.
Opened and closed checking and savings accounts; issued loan checks, moneyorders and travelers' checks; explained loan programs to customers.

Howard Johnson Hotel, Schiller Park, IL   1993-1994
Front Desk Supervisor
Handled all aspects of customer check-in/out, reservations and staff supervision. Effectively identified and resolved problem situations in a professional manner.
Prepared weekly staff work schedules. Approved all customer credits.

Holiday Inn, Des Plaines, IL   1991-1993
Reservations Manager
Assigned rooms to guests and managed space availability. Worked with major clients to negotiate and reserve blocks of rooms. Handled the billing for major accounts and Privilege Plus Members.

EDUCATION:

Harper College, Palatine, IL
Associate Degree in Business (in process)
Successfully completed nearly two years of credit toward degree. Relevant courses include Marketing, Management, French and Accounting.

166

RICHARD M. PLATE

771 Greenwood Court
Streamwood, IL 60107

630/555-1325

OBJECTIVE: **RESTAURANT MANAGEMENT**

- ▶ Skilled in promotions, menu planning, food presentation and customer service; effectively hire and supervise front-house and kitchen staff.

- ▶ Plan and conduct staff training and service review meetings to update and maintain customer service and quality goals.

EMPLOYMENT: Grisanti's Italian Restaurant, Schaumburg, IL   1993-1999
Manager
In charge of front-house and kitchen operations, with responsibility for staff scheduling, food presentation and customer service.
Assisted with accounting and office administration activities including P&L statement preparation, cash reconciliation and invoicing.
- → Conducted staff motivational and training meetings to set and achieve sales and customer service goals.
- → Handled all liquor ordering and inventory control.
- → Promoted to this position from **Server**, 8/93-6/95.

Naggy's Crab Cooker, Downers Grove, IL   1988-1993
Kitchen Manager
Responsible for production functions, including food/supply ordering, receiving, storing, preparation, equipment maintenance, facility cleanliness and sanitation.
Planned menus and formulated recipes working closely with chefs.
Hired, trained and supervised staff; reviewed performance.
- → Wrote and produced manuals on food preparation and handling procedures.
- → Designed and implemented a weekly physical inventory control system.

Bob Chinn's Crabhouse, Wheeling, IL   1983-1988
Kitchen Manager
- → Worked closely with the owner and managers to develop and implement this restaurant's concept following the opening in December 1982.
- → Assisted with inventory purchasing and control.
- → Developed PARS, expediter and Food Runner systems.

Cafe Benard, Northbrook, IL   1979-1983
Server
Gained initial experience in restaurant service and sales activities, working with a multi-national group of colleagues.

EDUCATION: J.B. Conant High School, Hoffman Estates, IL   Graduated 1979

NICK J. ROUTER

1224 Swift Commons, #501

Addison, IL 60101

708/555-8731

OBJECTIVE: *ROUTE SALES / ACCOUNT MANAGEMENT*

EXPERIENCE:

- Proven organizational and interpersonal communication skills to build rapport and positive relationships with customers, clients and the public.

- Familiar with retail food product route sales, delivery, order fulfillment and processing, as well as warehousing.

- Effectively train, supervise and motivate subordinates and peers to meet organizational goals.

- Extensive background in motor vehicle and aircraft parts customer service in support of maintenance, repair and fabrications.

EMPLOYMENT: Frito-Lay, Itasca, IL   1997-Present
Warehouse Team
Performed order filing, processing, stocking and shipping functions for retail food packaged products.

Brownberry Ovens, Glen Ellyn, IL   1995-1997
Order Processor
Handled order fulfillment, delivery and troubleshooting on retail food product routes to Chicago-area supermarkets.

Acorn Radiator Supply, Rosemont, IL   1992-1995
Managed an automotive and aircraft radiator supply and repair shop, including supervision and training of five technicians.
* Performed fabricating of tools and equipment used in the radiator maintenence field.

Don's Radiator Service, Carol Stream, IL   1981-1992
Shop Supervisor/Maintenance Technician
Performed all shop operations, including staff scheduling, supply ordering, and liaison with wholesale and distributor accounts.

Other recent employment: One year as a vehicle repair technician and part-time work as a deejay/musical coordinator for social and entertainment events.

EDUCATION: College of DuPage, Glen Ellyn, IL   1987-1988
Completed various courses in Electronics.

JULIE A. FINDER

2229 S. Troy
Posen, IL 60469
708/555-4586

OBJECTIVE: *SAFETY / LOSS PREVENTION:* A position where skills in loss control and/or government safety standards would be utilized.

PROFILE:
- ▶ Experience in property evaluations and the planning/implementation of safety and loss control programs, including full OSHA compliance.
- ▶ Train and supervise staff in on-the-job safety and loss prevention, including surveillance and apprehensions.
- ▶ Develop and analyze claims and medical reports; proven ability to determine and reduce dollar reserves and create light-duty, return-to-work programs.

EMPLOYMENT: **Loss Prevention Manager**
Montgomery Ward, Inc., Chicago, IL   11/89-Present
In charge of all loss control, security and safety procedures at this facility with 120 employees, including internal investigations and compliance to all OSHA standards.
Perform safety audits and evaluations to determine and solve chronic problems; conduct staff training in fire safety, first aid and overall worker safety.
Produce incident/medical reports for public liability and worker's compensation; work with doctor's offices and insurance companies.
- → Ranked #2 in internal investigations, 1991.
- → Interview injured persons and witnesses.
- → Promoted from Lombard and Bloomingdale locations.
- → Implement OSHA standards and plan/conduct safety training and evaluations for various departments.
- → Handle extensive group and individual training in all safety and loss control issues, and the latest OSHA standards; assist in staff hiring and supervision.

Graduate Assistant / Head Resident,
Southern Illinois University, Carbondale, IL   8/86-5/89
Managed a drug/alcohol and crisis intervention program.
Supervised 16 staff and emergency procedures for university housing.

Illinois State's Attorney, Marion, IL   1/87-5/87
Legal Assistant

EDUCATION: Southern Illinois University, Carbondale, IL   8/85-5/87
Bachelor Degree: Criminal Justice / Criminal Science

South Suburban College, South Holland, IL   8/83-8/85
Minor: Law Enforcement

MEMBERSHIPS: American Society for Industrial Security, American Red Cross; American Red Cross Certified First Aid Instructor.

CONSTANT SIGHT

3478 Regal Court
Roselle, IL 60172   708/555-0786

OBJECTIVE: *SECURITY / LAW ENFORCEMENT*

PROFILE:
- ▶ Skilled in general law enforcement procedures including patrol duty, surveillance and crowd/traffic control.

- ▶ Security Certified and trained in arrests and apprehensions, as well as fire arms, the PR24 and incident reporting; conversant in Italian.

EMPLOYMENT: Rosemont Police Department / Special Services, Rosemont, IL
Auxiliary Police Officer   1990-Present
Responsible for basic law enforcement at Rosemont Stadium and the Expo center, including crowd surveillance and control.
Perform visual and ID checks of minors attempting to purchase or use alcohol, during foot and vehicle patrols.
Ensure adherence to local village ordinances; utilize radios and all police equipment.
Assist the general public with various logistic and legal matters.
→ Compile and submit daily accident/incident reports.
→ Assist in the training and orientation of new officers.

Hyatt Regency O'Hare, Rosemont, IL
Security Officer   On Call, 1991-1993
Conducted foot patrols throughout this hotel to protect against vandalism and theft.
Checked IDs of persons leaving and entering the building.
Responded to reports of disturbances.
Issued keys to personnel in housekeeping, supplies and custodial engineering.

Paul Worth Company, Chicago, IL
Electrical Apprentice   1985-1991
Responsible for assembly and maintenance of electrical systems including circuit breakers, vacuum break panels and plug fuse panels.

Illinois Protection Plant, Melrose Park, IL
Security Officer   1987-1989

EDUCATION: Triton College, River Grove, IL
Earned two certificates for completion of 20- and 40- hour credit programs in Security and Fire Arms, 1987 and 1990.

Special Services Office, Rosemont, IL   1990-Present
Extensive training in police procedures.

Steinmetz High School, Chicago, IL   Graduate

Steve Earl

155 Coldspring Terrace
Coldspring, TX 77331   earlectron@aol.com   *409/555-5696*

SERVICE TECHNICIAN: ELECTRONICS

PROFILE:
- ▶ Comprehensive experience in all aspects of machine maintenance and service, including troubleshooting, component installation and circuit repair.

- ▶ Proven ability to identify problem areas, determine methods to correct and execute repairs quickly and accurately.

- ▶ Skilled in circuit board service; change clips, solder components, replace board tracers and perform diagnostic testing.

- ▶ Extensive background training others in over-the-road driving as well as machine repair.

EXPERIENCE: DDS Aggregates, Humble, TX   12/97-Present
Driver
Operate large vehicles for hauling sand and rock to freeway construction sites.

DuPre Transport, Camden, TX   3/97-11/97
Provided logistics services to Champion Paper Company.
→ Qualified as a driver trainer.
→ Top 3 in revenue production for the 1st and 2nd quarters of 1997.

Stevens Transport, Dallas, TX   12/94-2/97
Performed professional driving/logistics operations for clients throughout 48 states.
→ Trained students in all aspects of over-the-road driving.
→ Named Driver of the Month April 1996 and December 1996.

Circus-Circus / Slots-A-Fun Casino, Las Vegas, NV   7/85-11/94
Service Technician
Responsible for all aspects of maintaining and servicing electronic and electro-mechanical gaming devices.
Performed troubleshooting of failed equipment. Identified and implemented repair methods including circuit and component replacement.
→ Functioned as the swing shift Lead Mechanic. Coordinated and distributed all work assignments and supervised maintenance activities.

EDUCATION: Jesse Jones High School   **Graduate**

TRAINING: International Gaming Technology *Fortune I Video Service*
International Union of Operating Engineers *Electronics Competency*
Stevens Transport *Phase I - V Driver Trainer Program*

MIGUEL PACKAGE

22181 Betty Court
Bartlett, IL 60103

708/555-1922

OBJECTIVE: *SHIPPING / RECEIVING / WAREHOUSE OPERATIONS*
A position where self-motivation would be utilized.

EXPERIENCE:
- Skilled in driving forklifts and cherry pickers for stocking and truck loading and unloading.

- Operate automated wrappers and machines, including Insta-Pak equipment; skilled in the repair of automotive systems; strong mechanical aptitude.

- Coordinate the shipping and receiving of emergency orders.

EMPLOYMENT: Picker International Parts Organization, Wood Dale, IL   5/91-5/99
Parts Warehouseman
Responsible for prompt, accurate stocking of medical equipment and parts. Assisted in assembling shelves and organizing the entire warehouse. Provided customer service to service engineers and updated/maintained accurate inventories.
→ Implemented "Quality Driven Leadership" programs.
→ Completed company-sponsored seminars in: Quality Driven Leadership, Problem Solving Processes, Automated Inventory Systems and Customer Service.

Edward Don Company, North Riverside, IL   1/90-1/91
Warehouseman
Ensured proper picking and shipping of restaurant supplies.
Assisted staff in the shipping and receiving department.
→ Completed two month's training in efficiency, to meet company quality standards.

Glassman Glass, Chicago, IL   1/88-12/89
Installer
Ordered and installed auto and storefront glass to customer's specifications.
Provided customers with estimates and assisted in all shopwork and deliveries.
→ Completed company training in customer service.

EDUCATION: Chicago School of Auto Mechanics, Chicago, IL   **Certificate: 5/83**

Benito Juarez High School, Chicago, IL   **Graduated: 5/82**

Jeffrey W. Batter

2228 Unit Court
Hanover Park, IL 60103   630/555-7281

SPORTS OPERATIONS / MANAGEMENT

PROFILE:

▶ Experience in the promotion of sporting events and programs, including community relations, advertising and general PR for the Kane County Cougars.

▶ Background in creative design and development for promotional items, such as displays, handouts, posters and other promotional items.

▶ Skilled in marketing, sales, customer service and new business development, including account management and vendor relations.

EXPERIENCE:

(Most relevant first):

Kane County Cougars, Geneva, IL   Summer, 1996
Intern
Responsible for a wide range of promotional and game-day duties for this highly successful, minor league baseball team.
Involved in creating and developing promotional materials, such as booklets and pocket schedules, aimed at Chicago-area merchants and the general public.
Set up displays and oversaw contests, games and giveaways with major supermarkets to promote and increase attendance among children and families.
Assisted in general box office and ticketing sales.
Conducted door-to-door promotional visits to local area businesses.

* Attendance doubled from 3,000 to 6,000 during this time.
* Effectively trained and monitored all vendors and employees in food preparation and sales techniques.
* Selected as one of a five-member team to maintain the playing field for game day.

Town & Country Distributors, Itasca, IL   7/97-5/98
Merchandiser
Performed sales, direct customer service and merchandising of beverages, including creating, developing and using retail displays for all products.

Euclid Beverage, Inc., St. Charles, IL   5/98-Present
Sales Supervisor, promoted from **Merchandiser**
Oversee drivers and merchandisers in the delivery and sale of beverages to major independent and chain retailers.
Manage promotions, contests and games, including giveaways to increase sales.
Ensure prompt, accurate product deliveries, as well as product rotation.

EDUCATION:

Western Illinois University, Macomb, IL
Bachelor of Arts Degree: Individual Studies   Graduated 5/97
Concentration: Sports Management.

DONALD S. STOCKER

22317 Ridgewood
Bensenville, IL 60106

708/555-1577

OBJECTIVE: A clerical position where proven organizational skills would be utilized.

EXPERIENCE:
- ▸ Skilled in stocking, inventory control and parts expediting, including responsibility for order pulling and distribution.
- ▸ Experience with computer databases for tracking and ordering parts and supplies; handle phone communications in a professional manner.
- ▸ Assist in training and supervising staff in warehousing and order expediting; skilled in forklift driving and loading/unloading heavy equipment.

EMPLOYMENT:

Northwest Airlines, Chicago/O'Hare, IL   12/93-Present
Stocking / Inventory Control
Work closely with mechanics and quickly meet their needs for parts and systems used in aircraft repair.
Track and order parts through the company computer system and deliver them to hangers and job sites.
Drive forklifts and load/unload engines and parts quickly and safely.
Handle all aspects of stocking and inventory control.
- ➝ Promoted to this position from a part-time Equipment Service employee.
- ➝ Communicate with vendors, suppliers and technicians in a professional manner.

Stickler Premium Ostriches, Bensenville, IL   1993
Sales Representative
Conducted sales presentations to farmers and ranchers.

River Valley Cemetery, West Dundee, IL   1992-1993
Mt. Emblem Cemetery, Elmhurst, IL   1987-1991
Foreman / Groundskeeper
Trained and supervised three employees in all groundskeeping functions.
Operated backhoes, lawn mowers and snowplows.

Murphy's Installation, Bensenville, IL   1985-1987
Installer
Performed expert installation of cedar siding, including training and supervising up to 15 employees in various work crews.
Scheduled jobs and purchased material, while working with customers for high product quality.

Wilson Pet Supply, Wood Dale, IL   1980-1985
Dock Foreman
Supervised order picking, forklift driving and efficient warehouse operations.

EDUCATION: Fenton High School, Bensenville, IL   Graduate

Frank J. Steel

320 N. Harvard #E
Villa Park, IL 60181

630/555-1710

Steel Production

PROFILE:
- ▶ Skilled in production, manufacturing and shop work, including equipment repair, job scheduling and quality control.
- ▶ Hands-on experience in the operation and maintenance of machinery such as die cutters, sewing machines, band saws and packaging equipment.
- ▶ Fluent in Spanish and English; strong aptitude for learning new procedures quickly and accurately, with a sharp eye on safety; **Certified Forklift Driver.**

EXPERIENCE:

<u>Sea Converters Co.</u>, Addison, IL   1997-Present
Operations / Supervisor
Supervise a wide range of production operations for the manufacture of protective covers for industrial equipment, using metal, plastic, foam and paper materials.
Operate various manufacturing equipment and measure products for custom designs.
Process payroll and update/maintain accurate inventories.
Determine prices and selecte freight carriers; assisted in shipping and receiving.
* Schedule jobs and oversee quality control and product pricing.
* Ship samples to customers and solve problems with products and billing.

<u>Fore Supply</u>, Addison, IL   1990-1997
Warehouse Operations / Driver
Responsible for the safe, prompt delivery of supplies to approximately 20 golf clubs and health facilities per day.
Updated and maintained records on all deliveries throughout Chicago and the suburbs.
Assisted in training new drivers in all procedures.
* Involved in all major warehouse operations including stocking, stacking, packaging and inventory control.

<u>Snuzzo's Enterprise</u>, Gary, IN   1989-1990
Bartender / Customer Service
Duties included scheduling, inventory control and counting/balancing cash receipts.

Erdelac's Service Station, Merr, IN   1987-1989
Station Attendant

Shakey's Pizza & Buffet, Portage, IN   1985-1986
Supervisor
Trained and supervised staff in food preparation and customer service.

EDUCATION: <u>Portage High School</u>, Portage, IN   **Graduate: 1986**

ROBERT P. SHOPMAN

2225 McKool Avenue
Streamwood, IL 60107

708/555-9358

MOLDER / SHOP OPERATIONS

PROFILE:

▶ Comprehensive experience in production, supervision and quality control from setup to finish; thorough knowledge of plastic injection molding processes including close-tolerance molding.

▶ Skilled in a variety of injection materials and equipment including engineering grade plastics, hot stampers, sonic welders, and Van Dorn, Kawaguchi, New Britton, HPM and Toshiba 45-1,000 ton plastic injection molding machines; familiar with robotics.

▶ Interpret blueprints and work with technical, quality assurance and operations personnel at all levels for high-performance teamwork; proficient in conversational Spanish.

EMPLOYMENT:

Suncast Corporation, Batavia, IL   1994–Present
Supervisor, 2nd Shift
Responsible for 2nd shift plastic injection molding activities in the manufacture of lawn and garden products.
Schedule and monitor the performance of 70 machine operators, material handlers and foremen; submit daily production reports.
Provide on-the-job training in pulling raw materials, machine setup, maintaining run cycles, and problem identification.
Process payrolls and coordinate disciplinary actions with the union steward and plant manager.
→ Promoted from Foreman, 1/94–8/95.
→ Attended TQM training and participated on a Quest Team project.
→ Completed Paulsen injection molding training.

Various Manufacturers, Chicago, IL   1992-1994
Production Foreman
Accepted temporary assignments in production operations.

Basic Plastic Products, Bensenville, IL   1983-1992
General Foreman
Monitored and controlled run cycles, production-line changeovers, idle time, bottlenecks and lot sizes.
Programmed machine startup times, speed, heat and pressure settings.
Interfaced with customers and quality assurance staff to correct design flaws.
Tested and evaluate prototypes; assisted mold makers and quality control staff in developing new mold specifications.
→ Promoted from 1st and 3rd Shift Foreman, and Machine Operator.
→ Major customers included Motorola, Xerox, IBM and AT&T.

EDUCATION:

Lane Technical High School, Chicago, IL   Graduated 1979

PAMELA ANSWER

2277 College Green Drive
Elgin, IL 60123   847/555-4545

OBJECTIVE: **Switchboard / Customer Service**
A position utilizing proven abilities in administration, organization and customer service.

EXPERIENCE: ■ Comprehensive experience in all aspects of customer service, sales support and general office functions.

■ Handle customer inquiries and complaints, order processing, file maintenance and data entry/retrieval.

■ Conduct customer presentations in a professional manner; skilled at troubleshooting in high-pressure situations.

EMPLOYMENT: Crawford & Company, Schaumburg, IL   1994–1999
Receptionist / Switchboard
Greeted customers and answered questions on claims for worker's compensation; scheduled conferences and answered phone calls.
Performed data entry and assigned new work to adjusters.
Assisted in insurance billing and processing.

Locke Rental, Marianna, FL   1988–1992
Rental Agent
Responsible for a full range of sales and office duties, including lease documentation, collections, cash deposit transactions, tenant relations, typing and problem resolution.
Planned and conducted numerous customer tours of rental facilities.
Coordinated the repair and maintenance of all rental facilities.

Unimax Inc., Schaumburg, IL   1987–1988
Customer Service Representative
Handled sales, order processing and telephone communications, as well as data entry/retrieval and customer relations.
Trained new personnel in all company procedures.
Participated in many industry conventions as a salesperson and company representative; conducted many presentations.

EDUCATION: Elgin Community College, Elgin, IL   1997-Present
Attending Paralegal and liberal arts courses on a part-time basis.

Marianna High School, Marianna, FL   1985
Graduate
• Volunteer: local community program for Downs Syndrome adults and children.

WILLIE P. WHEELER

2235 Elk Trail
Carol Stream, IL 60188   708/555-7655

OBJECTIVE: A **Technician** position where proven analytical skills would be utilized.

PROFILE:
- ▶ Skilled in the repair and maintenance of Bantec and Opex systems, including the 5700 imaging system, 90690 reader/sorter with encoder, encoders and ink jet cartridges.
- ▶ Experience in computer repair and troubleshooting; utilize DOS, Windows, WordPerfect, Lotus and Excel.
- ▶ Perform data entry and retrieval with speed and accuracy; communicate with staff and customers in a professional manner.

EXPERIENCE: GE Capital Credit Services, Addison, IL   2/96-Present
Expeditor
Responsible for batch processing of checks through equipment listed above.
Perform key-in and stamping of checks for Ameritech; load MICR tapes, open envelopes and bundle checks for processing in a Banteck machine.

United Parcel Service, Inc., Addison, IL   4/96
Receiving
Responsible for the prompt unloading of all types of packages.

ABT Associates, Chicago, IL   2/95-11/95
Field Interviewer
Personally interviewed subjects in a government survey on drug use, including collection of laboratory test samples.
Performed beta testing of computer software and systems.
Coordinated job sites with government agencies for a drug study program.
Compiled and entered data on a computer system for modem transmission.
Assisted in public relations and staff training.

Radio Shack / Tandy Company, Norridge, IL   1984-1994
Sales Representative
Conducted sales presentations for a wide range of electronics.
Provided customer service and handled cash transactions.
Updated and maintained inventories on all product lines.

The Blueprint Shoppe, Chicago, IL   1986-1991
Distribution / Driver

Prior experience as A/V Technician and Set Designer.

EDUCATION: DeVry Institute of Technology, Chicago, IL
Extensive training toward Associate Degree in Applied Electronics Science

Carl Schurz High School, Chicago, IL   Graduated 1984

LINDA BOTHERS

2230 Fresno Court, Unit D
Hanover Park, IL 60103

630/555-2475

TELEPHONE MARKETING

PROFILE:

▶ Comprehensive experience in customer service, inter-department communications, telephone operations and inventory control gained during long-term employment with United Airlines and Dobbs International.

▶ Proven ability to meet customer needs, handle multiple priorities and perform effectively with co-workers.

EXPERIENCE:

Alta Villa Banquet Hall, Roselle, IL

Server   Part-time, 1999-Present
Provide complete customer service to guests attending banquet functions.
Work with up to 30 customers at a time.
Serve food and beverages and ensure all needs are met in a timely, professional manner.
→ Winner of Server of the Month award for outstanding performance.

Dobbs International, Schaumburg, IL   1994–1998

Interior Dispatcher
Responsible for a wide range of service functions for this company providing catering to United Airlines.
Handled several phone lines and updated passenger information, including meal requests, on the computer system.
Coordinated meal needs of last-minute passengers; worked with the reservations department on last-minute requests.
→ Distributed weekly payroll.

United Airlines   1985-1994

Load Flight Checker
Handled customer service and inventory control activities for United flights.
Responded to phone inquiries from customers.
Checked flight inventory for meals, beverages, desserts and related items; restocked inventory as needed.
→ Wrote employee work schedules for the following day.

EDUCATION:

J.B. Conant High School, Hoffman Estates, IL   Graduated 1985

KENNETH GEARS

224 Freeman
Streamwood, IL 60107   708/555-0390

OBJECTIVE: A position in the Tool and Die industry where proven hands-on skills in Wire EDM programming, setup and operation will be utilized.

EXPERIENCE:
- ▶ Full project management abilities include programming, production scheduling and reading/interpreting blueprints.

- ▶ Skilled in the operation of Charmilles-Andrew, Agie and Sodick machines; operate lathes, grinders, drill presses and milling machines.

- ▶ Handle a wide variety of dies including extrusion, progressive, and compound, as well as gears, molds, jigs and fixtures.

- ▶ Proficient in close tolerance work; specialize in "A" work; accurately convert metric measurements.

EMPLOYMENT: Sharp Metal Products, Elk Grove Village, IL   8/92-Present

Wire EDM Programmer / Operator
Program and operate up to five wire machines, some of which are handling a full work load 24-hours per day, for this contract tool and die company.
Responsible for troubleshooting and all maintenance work.
Double-check blueprints for accuracy and make corrections as necessary.
Able to program in 3-D and Advanced Conics.
- → Work with a wide range of dies and wire cutting projects within tight timeframes and budgets.

Richco Plastics, Chicago, IL   2/87-8/92
Tool Room Machinist
Learned to set up and operate wire machines with this extrusion die maker.

EDUCATION: William Rainey Harper College, Palatine, IL   1990
Completed Introduction to CNC Setup and Operation

Maine West High School, Des Plaines, IL   1980-1982
Apprenticeship Program

Prosser High School, Chicago, IL   Graduated 1979
Machine Shop

RALPH P. DENSON

229 Ivy Court
South Elgin, IL 60177   847/555-0774

TOOL AND DIE MAKER / PRODUCTION OPERATIONS

PROFILE:
- ▶ Extensive background in virtually all aspects of production line functions, with full responsibility for supervision of tool and die machining activities.
- ▶ Skilled in machining and assembly work for specialty jobs; interpret blueprints/schematics, and fabricate tools and dies in accordance with customer specifications; proficient in close tolerance work.
- ▶ Train and supervise shop personnel in parts production and modification, routine maintenance and daily cleanups; provide specific training in a wide range of dies including progressive and compound.

TECHNICAL KNOWLEDGE:
- *Milling/Grinding Machines:* vertical/digital readout Bridgeport machines; 516 Van Norman; six-twelve deluxe Boyar Schultz FSG-612 Chevalier Surface Grinder; Okamoto Automatic Feed Wet-Grinder (12x18) Table; Norton 10x18 Wet Grinder; familiar with the Moore Jig grinder.
- *Lathes:* 15x41 Tuda lathe; Hardinge Collet lathe.
- *Drill Presses:* American Radial w/automatic feed; Fosdick 3'x4" press; PowerMatic 4'x5' press.

EMPLOYMENT:
DEC Tool Corporation, Bensenville, IL   9/87-Present
Tool and Die Maker / Lead Journeyman
Supervise two apprentices in a wide range of shop procedures and fabrication of tool and die parts/components; provide on-the job training in equipment utilization, prevention maintenance and area cleanup; assign jobs and prepare status reports.
Visit customer sites to verify product fit; resolve problems promptly.
Order and inventory stock of all screws, dolls, nuts and bolts bi-monthly.
Maintain the tool crib and monitor tool/supply checkouts.
Perform routine repairs and regularly inspect tools for reconditioning.
- → Set up tryout dies in a 30-ton punch press with an automatic air feed and direct refinishing jobs.
- → In charge of all dies in absence of the plant manager.

Louisville Golf Club Company, Louisville, KY   5/81-8/87
Lead Assembler
Mill cut wood heads for insert, with quality responsibility for the production line from first task to finished product, with output up to 900 clubs per day.
- → Key corporate clients included Wilson and Austads Golf, and individual clients such as Eddie Mudd, Jodie Mudd and Andy North.

Smith & Silliaman, Louisville, KY   5/80-5/81
Laborer/Construction Crew

EDUCATION:
College of DuPage, Glen Ellyn, IL   1989-1992
Diploma, Apprentice School, Tooling Manufacturing Association

DEBORAH A. TRAFFIC

2219 Circle Drive
Roselle, IL 60172

Residence 847/555-2508
Office 847/555-5949

TRAFFIC COORDINATION

PROFILE:

▶ Extensive background in distribution, shipping/receiving and warehouse logistics, with attention to detail in fast-paced environments.

▶ Skilled in customer service, inventory tracking, expediting shipments and documentation; coordinate troubleshooting with carriers, distributors and sales personnel in a professional manner.

▶ Knowledge of various database and inventory control systems including AmCom, Walker and MB; proficient in Lotus 1-2-3; pursuing a course in WordPerfect 6.0.

EMPLOYMENT: AM Multigraphics, Inc., Mt. Prospect, IL   1985-Present
A manufacturer/distributor, with $204 million in annual worldwide sales.

Traffic Coordinator   4/95-Present

Responsible for the inbound/outbound logistics of shipping machines to customers, and receiving parts from suppliers and vendors.
Select truck lines, routes and rates according to purchase order requirements.
Interact with carriers to resolve problems including AAA, CCX and NW.
Trace and confirm shipments; prepare and analyze the weekly Transit Report to monitor actual time to deliver shipments.
Process documentation promptly including bills of lading and order confirmations.
Utilize Lotus to prepare and distribute numerous activity, control and billing reports.

→ Created a Lotus 1-2-3 table of machine weights by model and part numbers.

→ In charge of logistics for expediting heavy machines for display at trade shows including the Graph Expo '95 show at McCormick Place.

Data Control Clerk   8/85-4/95

Processed confirmation for shipments and open-order paperwork, including accurate and rapid data entry and report generation; identified and resolved discrepancies.

Picker Intn'l Medical Equipment & Supplies, Wood Dale, IL   8/84-8/85
Customer Service Clerk

Filled and processed telephone purchase orders including parts identification, stock availability and shipping/merchandise problems, working with the Purchase Department.

→ Attended an Illinois Bell seminar on customer service.

Homemaker   1982-1984

AM Multigraphics, Inc., Elk Grove Village, IL
Group Leader, Inventory Control   1974-11/82

Trained and supervised up to five CRT operators in accurately processing an average of 1,000 work orders daily; trained on the Cullinet System; maintained the equipment.

→ Promoted to this position from Data Control Clerk in 1978.

EDUCATION: Driscoll Catholic High School, Addison, IL   Graduated 1974

RICHARD NETTER

2206 Beverly Lane
Streamwood, IL 60107   708/555-0339

OBJECTIVE:	**Transportation Operations:**

A position where proven skills would be utilized.

EXPERIENCE:

- More than seven years in freight routing and distribution, including full responsibility for LTLs, truckloads and ocean shipments.

- Handle claims processing and negotiate rates and contracts in a cost-effective manner with major carriers; plan and implement policies, procedures and special projects.

- Utilize Lotus Spreadsheet 2.3, Officewriter, Q&A Database, ProComm, FastBack and QDOS 3 for general accounting, freight accruals, chargebacks correspondence and reports.

EMPLOYMENT:

Boise Cascade Office Products, Itasca, IL   5/86–Present
Administrative Technician   9/91–Present
A wide range of duties include policy/procedure planning, claims processing and transportation analysis for inbound and outbound freight. Negotiate rates for LTL, truckload and small package carriers. Create and maintain database files for contracts and insurance certificates.
* Familiar with hazardous material regulations (HAZMAT).

Administrative Analyst I   7/90–8/91
Managed the entire freight consolidation program, including monthly freight accruals, routing and accounting statements.
Trained and supervised two employees in customer service, freight coding and claims processing.
Controlled line haul activity into 33 distribution centers.
Audited freight bills and negotiated rates.
* Controlled up to $4.7 million annually in inbound freight expense; approximate tonnage: 7 million pounds.
* Automated the billing process using Lotus and controlled a computerized freight chargeback program.
* Controlled up to 40 truckloads per week, as well as annual catalog distribution.

Administrative Specialist IV   5/86–6/90
Performed manual rating of bills of lading for the chargeback program.

Prior Experience with
Kraft Foods Accounting Center as Credit Specialist and Data Entry Clerk.

EDUCATION:
Completed extensive training in freight claims processing and quality control through Boise Cascade. High school graduate.

RENCE M. USIK

2833 E. Fairfield Court
Lombard, IL 60148

630/555-8689

OBJECTIVE: *TRANSPORTATION / DELIVERY SERVICES*
Distribution Operations

PROFILE:
- ▶ Experience in shipping/receiving and parcel/freight expediting activities, including unloading/loading, load balancing, productivity troubleshooting and problem resolution, with supervisory responsibilities.

EMPLOYMENT: RPS / Caliber System, Inc., Bedford Park, IL   7/96-Present
Package Sort Coordinator Rotate between two assignments on a regular basis:
Control Room Coordinator Perform dock/yard troubleshooting activities and control throughput productivity, including load balancing, pace determination and sorter downtime, utilizing an AS/400 system and T.V. monitors.
- → Direct the flow between unload/destination areas by radio and telephone.
- → Contact maintenance personnel to resolve electrical and equipment problems.

Unload Coordinator Train and supervise up to 20 package handlers per shift in daily shipping/receiving activities, including sort prioritization.
Key Accomplishments
- → Certified in first aid by the American Red Cross.
- → Set company Hub records for largest volume per hour throughput.

United Parcel Service, Hodgkins, IL   1995-1996
Yard Control Clerk   12/95-7/96
Coordinated all international parcel mailing/delivery service activities, with responsibility for 30-35 loads, dispatching requests to outbounds and balancing optimal usage of equipment.
Handled the stripping/respotting of trailers on primary/outbound location.
- → Set up for next shift sort and dispatched hot cut-offs to the rail yard.

Dispatch Clerk   9/95-12/95
Dispatched inbound/outbound trailers and assigned loads to drivers.
Called other UPS distribution locations to expedite shipments and check the availability/location of equipment.
- → Logged arrival times for shipments during the Sunrise Sort shift.

Global Intelligence, Itasca, IL   6/95-8/95
Research Analyst
Identified up to 30 applicants per available position, for client recruiters.

EDUCATION: Western Illinois University, Macomb, IL   Graduated 5/95
B.A. degree in public communication/human relations
Minor: Human Resources Management

College of DuPage, Glen Ellyn, IL   Graduated 6/93
Associate Applied Science degree in liberal arts

CAROL FLIGHTBOOK

22161 Avalon Court
Roselle, IL 60172

630/555-7917

TRAVEL AGENT

PROFILE:

▸ Successful experience in all agency procedures, including sales and customer service for domestic and international airline tickets, cruises and hotel/car packages for groups and individuals.

▸ Skilled in Apollo for itinerary planning, price quoting, ticketing and confirmations; familiar with Windows 95, WordPerfect and Lotus for account updating, status reporting and correspondence.

RELEVANT EXPERIENCE:

Main Street Travel, West Chicago, IL   1994-1999
Corporate Travel Agent
Responsible for training and supervising two employees in all agency operations for corporate accounts, including outside group reservations for worldwide travel.
Worked closely with accounts and suggested and booked carrier rates and routes, hotel accommodations, car rentals and entertainment packages.
* Conducted sales, customer service and bookings with personal touch, often under strict deadlines.

We-Go Travel, West Chicago, IL   1991-1994
Leisure Agent
Utilized Apollo and various systems to book flights and all related accommodations for leisure travel, primarily for small corporations, groups and individuals.
Booked air, hotel and car reservations, while suggesting locations and accommodations; ensured accuracy of all ticketing.
* Developed a referral clientele through attention to detail and followup.

Banque Travel, Oakbrook Terrace, IL   1985-1991
Corporate Agent
Gained experience booking all major travel services for corporate accounts.
Updated and maintained records and profiles of key accounts.

CURRENT POSITION:

Federal Express, Inc., Naperville, IL   1996-Present
Courier
Responsible for on-time pickups and deliveries of packages to business and residential locations.

EDUCATION:

Maki Travel School, Downers Grove, IL
Completed 108 hours of workshop training in all phases of Travel and Agency Operations, including 30 hours of computer training.

College of DuPage, Glen Ellyn, IL
Degree: Business Administration Major: Accounting

SONIA SPINNER

2213 Nautilus
Hanover Park, IL 60103   708/555-6681

THE TRAVEL INDUSTRY
A position with an agency or tour operator, where professional skills would be utilized.

PROFILE:
> ▶ Proven abilities in all agency operations including ticketing, itinerary planning, bookings and effective customer service.

> ▶ Utilize Apollo and Sabre; handle price quotes and domestic/international bookings with a strong knowledge of routes, rates and carriers.

> ▶ Professionally handle customer communications; familiar with German.

EMPLOYMENT: United Express, O'Hare Airport, Chicago, IL   9/86–9/93 and 4/94–1/95
Operations Agent
Responsible for various airport and ramp operations, including updating passenger flight information, on the APOLLO system.
Involved in determining aircraft weights and balances.

Ramp Agent: Loaded and unloaded planes with both cargo and passengers.
Interlined baggage and worked in the bag room.

Travel Technology, Wheaton, IL   2/94–4/94
Corporate Travel Agent

Kwality Travel, Bloomingdale, IL   9/93–1/94
Travel Agent
Performed price quoting, ticketing and customer service on the SABRE system.

Midstate Airlines, Stevens Point, WI   6/84–8/86
State / Ticket Agent, Gate & Operations Agent
Utilized SABRE and tracked lost luggage; handled bag room and ramp agent duties.

EDUCATION: Southeastern Academy, Kissimmee, FL
Diploma   1983
Trained in travel industry operations including OAG (domestic and international), domestic tariffs, ticketing, tours, cruises, hotel/motel booking, car rental, travel markets, programmed airline reservations systems and salesmanship.

College of DuPage, Glen Ellyn, IL   9/81–5/83
Studied travel, speech, English, composition, data processing, management, auto maintenance and German.

Addison Trail High School, Addison, IL   Graduated 1981

MELVIN BURNER

225 Elm Court #8
Hanover Park, IL 60103   630/555-9447

WELDER / FABRICATOR

EXPERIENCE:
- ▸ Skilled in all types of welding including mig, tig, gas, stick and plasma for custom fixtures and finished products.

- ▸ Natural talent for innovation and fixture design; maintain strict quality standards, as well as shop safety and cleanliness.

- ▸ Trained in lathes, mills, drills and polishers; personally own more than $2,500 worth of hand tools.

- ▸ Communicate well with management, co-workers and customers as needed; assist in worker training in welding procedures.

EMPLOYMENT: **WELDER / FABRICATOR** at the following locations:

Flex-Weld, Bartlett, IL   6/96-Present
Responsible for all types of fixture welding including mig-tig welding of stainless to carbon steel.
Work within strict tolerances; perform welding of metal .005 to 1/4 inches.
Involved in the fabrication of precision bellows (with EPEJ's and EJ's) for HVAC applications.
Maintain excellent cleanliness and safety of work areas.

Colony Display, Hanover Park, IL   1995-1996 and 1993-1994
Performed all types of welding for a wide range of products.
Utilized customer's blueprints and assembled display racks and fixtures for such accounts as Wal-Mart, Home Depot and Eveready.

Precision Quincy, Woodstock, IL   1994-1995
Responsible for precision welding of industrial ovens and dryers.

Lake Process, Barrington, IL and AEC, Inc., Wood Dale, IL   1992-1994
Welded cooling tanks used in plastic injection molding.
Assembled stainless steel equipment, often using purge/tig, free-hand and out-of-position welding.

EDUCATION:
Elgin Community College, Elgin, IL   Present
Completed 39 of 60 credits towards Associate Degree in Welding.

Dundee Crown High School, Carpentersville, IL   GED: 1991

PERSONAL: Highly self-motivated, reliable and quality-conscious.

DARRELL N. BLAZER

2252 Winding Glen Drive
Carol Stream, IL 60188   708/555-5192

OBJECTIVE: **Maintenance Welder**
A position where professional skills would be utilized.

EXPERIENCE:
- Proficient in all types of welding including MIG, TIG, ARC, Flux-core and Acetylene.

- Skilled in fabricating industrial and commercial products, using stainless steel, aluminum and brass.

- Train and supervise shop personnel in a wide range of operations; handle spot welding, press brakes, punch presses and sheet metal rollers.

EMPLOYMENT: <u>Custom Enclosures,</u> Elmhurst, IL   3/93-Present
Welder
Responsible for all duties listed above as well as shipping and receiving at this custom sheet metal fabrication shop.
Weld enclosures, steel columns and sound-proof panels.
Perform electrostatic spray painting and track time requirements for specific projects.

<u>Diamond Automation,</u> Farmington Hills, MI   7/89-3/93
Welder / Fabricator
Welded and assembled specialty packing equipment using MIG, TIG & Gas welders.
Responsible for a wide range of maintenance welding throughout the plant.

<u>Perimeter Security,</u> Miami, FL   1/87-7/89
Manager / Owner
Hired, trained and supervised up to 4 employees in the welding, assembly and installation of gates and aluminum fences.
Involved in budget planning, payroll and direct customer service.

<u>York Corrugating,</u> York, PA   5/78-1/87
Welder / Fabricator
Performed a wide range of production work for Mack and Peterbilt trucks.

<u>Rockland Manufacturing, Inc.,</u> Bedford, PA   2/76-5/78
Welder / Fabricator & Supervisor
Trained and supervised up to 7 employees in field repair, welding and maintenance of equipment including bulldozer blades and buckets.

EDUCATION: <u>High School Graduate</u>
Successful completion of welding classes.

JOSEPH NICHOLSON

2206 South State Street
Elgin, IL 60123

847/555-8017

WAREHOUSING / DISTRIBUTION MANAGEMENT

PROFILE:

▶ Extensive experience in all aspects of warehousing, including management of facilities up to 500,000 square feet.

▶ Supervise management and hourly employees in both union and non-union environments.

▶ Skilled in shipping, receiving, warehousing, inventory control and company fleet coordination.

▶ Pioneered a Material Handling System: RF environment with 100% positive inventory tracking of product (Panasonic).

→ Worked closely with programmers and systems designers to redesign inventory/ warehouse management system (Panasonic).
→ Trained all levels of employees, hourly and management, on system-driven environments, bar coding, RF systems, etc.

▶ Proven ability to achieve specific goals and improve operations.

→ Boosted productivity standards in all positions.
→ Improved morale in all positions, leading to increased productivity.

EXPERIENCE:

Vallen Safety Supply Company, **Warehouse Supervisor,** August 1995 - Present

Preferred Meal Systems, **Warehouse Manager,** January 1994 - July 1995

Panasonic, **Assistant Manager,** September 1990 - January 1994

Quality Distribution, **Warehouse Manager,** September 1985 - September 1990

Wayco Foods Corporation, **Night Superintendent,** October 1982 - September 1985

EDUCATION: Morton College: Completed one year of Business Administration program.

United States Marine Corps School of Supply Administration.
Completed various seminars conducted by ASMI and AMA.

MILITARY: E-4 Supply Administration, U.S. Marine Corps, 1980-1982.

ANDREW CLAMPER

Postage: P.O. Box 31
Bensenville, IL 60106

708/555-3670

Res: 1054 W. Irving Pk Rd.
Bensenville, IL 60106

OBJECTIVE: A position where skills in Warehousing and/or Plant operations would be utilized.

EXPERIENCE:

- More than seven years in shipping, receiving and distribution, including forklift driving, order picking and stocking.

- Experience in computerized order tracking and form preparation, labeling and the packing of rail cars and semi-trailers.

- Operate factory equipment including clamp trucks and boom lifts.

EMPLOYMENT: Nexxus Distributors, Schaumburg, IL   1989-1999
Warehouse Clamp Operator
Responsible for safely driving a clamp truck to load/unload large paper rolls, zinc ingots and pallets on semi-trailers and rail cars.
Supervise two employees in shipping/receiving and the writing of order forms on the computer system.
Handled stocking, order pulling and warehouse maintenance at this major facility.

Cincinnati Steel, Elk Grove Village, IL   1988-1989
Shop Labor
Performed shipping, receiving and routing; wrote and filled orders.
Operated a bandsaw and ensured quality of material dimensions, paint color and color codes.

Carson Pirie Scott & Co., Elk Grove Village, IL   1987-1988
Warehouseman
Operated a carpet boom/forklift for the pulling and stocking of large rolls of carpet.
Responsible for product labeling, wrapping and stocking.

Ramsey Popcorn, Ramsey, IN   1982-1986
Cleaner / Operator
Worked with a variety of factory machinery.
Efficiently packaged and loaded products.

MILITARY: U.S. Army, **Combat Engineer**   1977-1981

Davea Center, Addison, IL   1976-1977
Certificate: Construction and Electrical Wiring.

Fenton High School, Palatine, IL   Graduated 1977

DARYL MAKER

227 Altgeld
Glendale Heights, IL 60139

630/555-5472

WAREHOUSING / PRODUCTION

PROFILE:

▶ Comprehensive experience in a wide range of steel production and warehouse functions including crane operations, loading, machining and torch cutting.

▶ Trained in hem saw operations to cut steel within tight tolerances. Proficient with a variety of tools such as saws, air guns, power tools and scales.

▶ Licensed and highly skilled forklift driver; operate electric, gas and propane powered lifts including stand-ups and high-lifts. Proficient crane operator.

EXPERIENCE:

Triple S Steel, Houston, TX   1/97-1/99
Warehouseman
Responsible for all aspects of stock movement, inventory control and truck loading.
Operated cranes to handle the movement and loading of steel products.
→ Performed torch cutting and hem saw operations; cut steel products to customer specifications.

Compaq Computers, Houston, TX   5/96-11/96
Material Handler
Operated a forklift to pull stock from inventory and deliver to production/assembly lines.
Unloaded trucks and restocked inventory.

Nippon Express, Wood Dale, IL   2/90-4/96
Forklift Operator
Unloaded trucks, loaded 20- and 40-foot containers for sea shipment and restocked inventory.
Utilized various power tools, saws and air guns; worked with the crating department.

Express Fasteners, Glendale Heights, IL   4/87-1/90
Plater
Entered material movements in the computer. Operated forklifts and used scales for various warehouse functions.

EDUCATION:

Glenbard North High School, Carol Stream, IL
Graduated 1984

GEORGE X. RAYMOND

123 N. Addison Road
Addison, IL 60101   708/555-3916

OBJECTIVE: **X-Ray Technician / Radiology**
A position requiring skills in patient diagnosis and personalized care.

EXPERIENCE:
- Comprehensive experience in radiology and clinical care, including mammography; utilize C-arm, GE, OEC and Siemens equipment, as well as mobile units.

- Proficient in general diagnostics including fluoroscopy, UGI and LGI, osteopathic and T-Tube cholangiography, tamography-axial and appendicular; experience in trauma cases.

EMPLOYMENT: Northlake Hospital, Melrose Park, IL   1/90–4/99
Staff Technologist
Responsible for a full range of general radiology and direct patient care, including the majority of procedures listed above.
This 280-bed hospital includes an extensive outpatient facility.
Worked effectively with physicians, nurses and technical staff at all levels.
* Utilized a CRT and conducted patient reception/scheduling in a personalized, yet professional manner.
* Experienced with portable traumas, pacemakers, angiograms and line placements.

Mercy Center, Aurora, IL   1983–1986
Pharmacy Technologist
Accurately filled prescriptions; gained a strong knowledge of drugs and interactions.
Conducted pharmacy inventories and verified/maintained orders and patient records.

ACCREDITATION: American Registry of Radiologic Technologists   Registered 11/89–11/92
Illinois Department of Nuclear Safety   License: 10/89–10/93

CERTIFICATIONS: *   **Certified** in CPR; **Certified** Pharmacy Technician

EDUCATION: College of DuPage, Glen Ellyn, IL   1989
A.A.S. Degree   Graduated with High Honors: 3.9/4.0
* Continuing Education Points: 35, including 14 in Mammography.

Hines VA Hospital, Chicago, IL   One Month, 1989
Trained in Special Procedures and clinical applications.

Delnor Community Hospital, Geneva and St. Charles, IL   1987–1989
Clinical Experience

MEMBERSHIPS: American Association of Radiologists and Technologists
Illinois Society of Radiologic Technologists

Resumes for Entry-level Office, Management and Technical Positions

BERNICE PAYER

9422 South Broad Street
Scottsboro, AL 35768

847/555-9877

ACCOUNTS PAYABLE / BOOKKEEPING

PROFILE:

▶ Skilled in AP/AR, journal entries, general ledger maintenance, payroll processing, quarterly tax returns and financial statement preparation.

EMPLOYMENT: Marriott Hotel Corporation, Elmhurst, IL   8/95-6/99
Night Auditor / Front Desk Clerk
Greeted customers, verified reservations, assigned rooms and handled problems.
Performed all aspects of daily audit procedures, including the reconciliation of food/beverage and guest statistic accounts.
Forecasted daily, weekly and monthly occupancy rates.
Reviewed, updated and adjusted budgets; produced the monthly and fiscal year-end budget variance reports.

West Suburban Currency Exchange, Wood Dale, IL   4/96-9/96
Cashier / Part-time
Accepted and handled a wide range of state-authorized financial transactions, including check cashing, money orders, vehicle plate, sticker and title issuance, food stamps and Western Union telegrams/moneygrams.
Opened/closed the cash drawer, reconciled deposits and deposited receipts daily.

Affordable Closet, Roselle, IL   3/88-3/96
Bookkeeper
Responsible for prompt, accurate processing of all billing, payroll and quarterly tax returns for this designer of custom shelving systems; handled AP/AR matters.
Scheduled appointments and quoted prices to customers in a professional manner.
→ Produced profit/loss statements and reconciled bank accounts.

**PRIOR
EXPERIENCE:** A&P Tea Company, Chicago, IL
Store Managers' Trainer / Head Cashier
Trained and assisted store managers throughout Chicagoland in general accounting, bank deposit procedures and cash flow analysis; analyzed cash flow and compiled/presented weekly status reports to headquarters.

EDUCATION: Northwestern University, Evanston, IL
Completed a two-year program in accounting.

ROZ HALIBURTON

8789 Limerick Lane
Schaumburg, IL 60193

847/555-9158

OBJECTIVE: A position where office administration, communication and computer skills would be utilized.

PROFILE:
- ▶ Comprehensive skills in office administration including operations, scheduling and customer relations.
- ▶ Proficient in Windows 95 and WordPerfect 6.0; familiar with Lotus 1-2-3; utilize various office equipment efficiently including copiers, facsimile machines, calculators and computers.
- ▶ Skilled in accounts payable, payroll, writing correspondence, switchboard operations, data entry/retrieval and communications.

EMPLOYMENT: Century 21 All Professionals, Glen Ellyn, IL   12/94-3/96
Administrative Assistant
Provide administrative support to various companies in the metropolitan Chicago area.
- · Write correspondence utilizing WordPerfect 6.0 for Windows.
- · Handle telecommunications and greet clients.
- · Update and prepare scheduled/on-demand reports.

Homemaker   11/92-12/94

Dutkovich Properties, Hoffman Estates, IL   1/91-11/92
Administrative Assistant
Performed various office duties for this property management company including record keeping, customer service, correspondence and credit checks.
- · Scheduled a maintenance crew of up to six members; distributed payment checks.
- · Greeted renters and resolved complaints.

Olsten Temporary Services, Schaumburg, IL   5/88-10/89
Secretary / Accounts Payable Clerk
Provided a wide range of services including accounts payable, data entry/ retrieval, word processing and office administration.

Motorola, Inc., Schaumburg, IL   7/84-5/88
Payroll Clerk
Compiled and maintained current payroll records; entered and retrieved data on computer.
Verified payroll codes/hours and distributed weekly paychecks.

EDUCATION: College of DuPage, DuPage, IL
WordPerfect 6.0 for Windows course   1/95-3/95

District 211 Continuing Education Program   1992
Completed Lotus 1-2-3

LARRY CAPP

2441 Player Lane
North Beach, CA 34560   212/555-5892

ADMINISTRATION / MANAGEMENT

PROFILE:
- Skilled in human relations, staff training and motivation; well-versed in group dynamics and processes.

- Conduct written and oral presentations in a professional manner; organize meetings, programs and events.

- Hands-on experience in vendor relations, customer service and sales; write and distribute correspondence; coordinate budgets and business operations.

EDUCATION: University of Illinois, Urbana-Champaign, IL
Bachelor's Degree, Major: Psychology   Graduated 5/98
* Pledge class Social Chairman: Delta Upsilon Fraternity.

Elgin Community College, Elgin, IL
Activities required extensive human relation, motivation and organizational skills:
* Elected to ECC's College Community Council, representing the student body among various community groups and the general public.
* Represented ECC at various conferences: NACA, ACUI and ICCSAA.
* Served as coordinating Vice President for the Student Senate.
* Co-founder of first Phi Alpha Delta pre-law fraternity at any Junior College.
* Awarded Leadership Scholarship for two consecutive years.
* Attended numerous leadership seminars.

EMPLOYMENT: The Gap, Elgin, IL   11/97-pesent
Sales Associate
Handled direct customer service, sales and inventory control.
* Ranked #3 in sales of 26 Associates in the first month.

The Sealmen, Bartlett, IL   Summer, 1997
Co-Owner
Hired, trained, motivated and supervised four employees.
Responsible for marketing, sales promotions and professional customer relations.

UNO's Pizza, Bartlett, IL   Summer, 1996
Shift Leader
Trained and supervised several employees in sales and all store operations.

Overhead, Inc., Chicago, IL   Summers & Breaks, 6/93-12/95
Inventory Control Clerk
Placed incoming equipment and supplies; assisted in shipping and receiving.
Tracked sales and configured a computerized vendor system.

DON JORDAN

2345 Whispering Oak Drive
Palatine, IL 60074

847/555-8658

ADMINISTRATION / MANAGEMENT

PROFILE:

▸ Extensive experience in customer service, sales and general office activities, including cash management and procedure development.

▸ Effectively train, motivate and supervise staff to meet established goals; plan and conduct training sessions.

▸ Skilled in inventory control and in-store merchandising; familiar with Word, WordPerfect, Lotus and Excel for data analysis and report preparation.

EXPERIENCE:

Circuit City Stores Inc., Schaumburg, IL — 1994-Present
Customer Service Lead — 1995-Present

Responsible for all daily activities in the Customer Service department of this high-volume retailer of computers and all major consumer electronics.

Train staff in departmental operations including total customer satisfaction, procedures and the in-house computer system.

Submit and record credit applications; document and manage files for all repair work.

Track and control parts inventory through the entire supply chain; follow up with customers.

* Improved part order collection rate from 40% to 90%, providing annual savings of $30,000; researched, documented and trained staff on correct procedures.

* Twice earned the "Hero" award for outstanding customer service.

Retail Sales Associate — 1994-1995

Worked with customers to identify and meet their individual needs and expectations for consumer electronics.

Acquired a detailed knowledge of product features and benefits.

Schaumburg Park District, Schaumburg, IL — 1988-1996
Pool Manager — 1995-1996

Managed daily operations of the recreational facility.

Responsible for scheduling employees and lifeguard post rotations to ensure proper coverage.

Planned and presented daily training sessions on topics such as emergency procedures, CPR, First Aid and lifesaving.

Life Guard — 1988-1995 (Summers)

Provided for the safety of facility patrons.

Coached several junior swim teams and gave swim instruction.

EDUCATION:

Roosevelt University, Chicago, IL
B.S. in Actuarial Science in progress; extensive coursework in mathematics and statistics. GPA: 3.4/4.0.

Harper College, Palatine, IL
A.S. Degree, Liberal Studies

SIMON MAKER

3412 N. Ash
Wood Dale, IL 60191   708/555-1982

OBJECTIVE: **ASSEMBLER / PROGRAMMER**

EXPERIENCE:
- Proven abilities in equipment assembly and the programming of PROMS, chips, bits and disks.

- Skilled in soldering and the use of power hand tools for building PC power units and NC/robotic systems to blueprints and specifications.

- Fluent in English and German; self-motivated and energetic, with a sharp eye for detail and quality.

EMPLOYMENT: Siemens, Erlangen, Germany   9/89-12/98
Assembler
Responsible for the prompt, accurate assembly of power units for PCs and NC and robotic devices to job specifications.
Handled extensive soldering and board swapping, as well as mounting and setup of machine tool controls.
Conducted accurate programming of PROMS, bits, disks and chips; numeric power units include the 810, 820, 840, 850 and 880.
Utilized all types of power tools; soldered PC boards for bridge connections.
* Performed final assembly and packaging of Simo drive systems.
* Updated notes on job orders for high-quality work.

Quelle, Erlangen, Germany   1987-1989
Order Processor
Duties included order picking, sorting and shipping for this catalog sales warehouse.

Vad & Fry, Erlangen, Germany   1985-1987
Assembler
Involved in high-quality clothing production.
Assisted in training one employee in pattern placement on fixating machinery.

Ramada/Renaissance Hotel, Aurora, CO   1985
Housekeeper
* Awarded Certificate for Most Conscientious Worker.

Army & Air Force Exchange Service, Aurora, CO   1982-1985
Sales Representative
Performed retail sales and direct customer service in a professional manner.
* Certified for completing a course in Human Relations.

EDUCATION: High School Graduate Degree / Equivalent, West Germany

NANCI TALKER

225 Santa Clara Street
Vallejo, CA 94590

707/555-7050

COUNSELING / RECOVERY

PROFILE:

▸ Extensive experience in case management, group/individual counseling and facilitation, including positive parenting and full responsibility for curriculum planning.

▸ Skilled in teaching 12-step recovery concepts; Certified to teach informational anti-smoking programs covering sociological trends, advertising and chemical dependency.

▸ Background in behavior modification, re-entry work and client sponsoring, as well as documentation and the design of custom treatment plans for individual clients, physicians and court cases; CPR and First Aid qualification.

▸ Personally establish rapport with people of all ages and philosophies, with a long-standing commitment to recovery; prioritize, motivate and delegate people in team settings; skilled in documentation, research and detailed report writing.

EXPERIENCE:

Our Family Inc., Napa, California   1995-Present

On-Call, Counselor

Responsible for personal counseling and supervision of up to 10 adults with various addictions, from screening and intake interviews to long-term treatment.

Coordinate 12-step orientation and act as the client's liaison to judicial, job training and social service agencies for comprehensive treatment.

Compile and present extensive written and oral reports, including case narratives for supervisors, social services, families and judicial systems.

Perform group facilitation for parenting, processes and therapeutic community activities.

* Personally established the 12-step curriculum, including all training of recovering, non-recovering and on-call staff.

* Founded the first positive parenting support program for the adult population.

* Formerly in charge of up to 15 adult clients and 7 juvenile clients.

VOLUNTEER:

Solano Alano Club, Vallejo, California   1993-1995

Director. Involved in financial and operational decisions; assisted in record keeping, inventory and advertising.

Solano Partnership Health Plan, Vallejo, California   1992

Consumer Advocate. Served on an informational board that assisted the State of California in the reconstruction of the MediCal benefit program.

Southern Solano Alcohol - S.S.A.C.   1989-1990

Staff Assistant. Adhered to policies and procedures, codes of ethics and laws regarding confidentiality. Performed crisis intervention and community referrals and collection of statistical data; assisted clinical staff.

EDUCATION:

Napa Valley College
Correctional Officer Certification

CONNI M. FILMER

220 West Roscoe #1N
Chicago, IL 60657   *312/555-5669*

FILM / TELEVISION PRODUCTION ASSISTANT

EXPERIENCE:

- Proven abilities as assistant to executives in production, home video and business administration.

- Experience with such companies as Warner Bros., Hanna-Barbera and Twentieth Century Fox.

- Skilled in office operations and department activities; knowledge of WordPerfect and Lotus 1-2-3.

- Plan and conduct written and oral presentations in a professional manner.

EMPLOYMENT: Hanna Barbera Productions, Hollywood, CA   8/91-6/99
Assistant to the Executive Producer
Planned and coordinated numerous aspects of production, including synopsis preparation and manuscript reading.
Coordinated writers, editors and producers of an animated TV series in collaboration with the Executive Producer.
* Provided additional support as needed to the Senior Vice President.

Twentieth Century Fox Film Corporation, Century City, CA
Temp. Assignment   6/91-7/91
Assistant to V.P. and General Counsel
See description of 4/89-5/90, below.

Warner Bros., Burbank, CA   5/90-5/91
Assistant to V.P. and General Counsel
(Warner Home Video)
Managed an entire Home Video Department in direct collaboration with the General Counsel.
Researched, prepared and drafted all agreements related to domestic and international home video distribution.
* Directed and organized virtually all office support functions.

Twentieth Century Fox Film Corporation, Century City, CA   4/89-5/90
Executive Assistant / Contract Administrator to the V.P. and Deputy General Counsel
Drafted contracts for talent and production staff, as well as option notice reports and contract status reports.
* Designed and improved administrative and office management procedures for the department.

EDUCATION: Glen Oaks Community College, Glen Oaks, CA   1988-1989
English Major

Becker G. Stylish   *(Chronological Resume)*
2247 Wentworth Lane
Bartlett, IL 60103
708/555-2348

EXPERIENCE: ***Graphic Designer***   2/92-Present
Associated Stationers, Itasca, IL
Responsible for the layout, design and production of consumer office
product catalogs and various promotional materials from concept through
press proof.
Proficient in QuarkXpress; familiar with Adobe Illustrator, Adobe
Photoshop and Microsoft Word.
  · Conceptualize, lay out and art direct catalog covers.
  · Design corporate signage for branch locations.

Graphic Design Specialist   1/88-1/92
Boise Cascade Office Products, Itasca, IL
Developed page layouts for wholesale consumer product catalogs.
Worked with pressroom staff on four-color projects.
Coordinated product photography.
Designed and art directed numerous dealer catalog covers.
  · Developed and produced an eight-page catalog insert for recycled
    products, 1992.
  · Produced the top selling and standard covers for wholesale and
    consumer catalogs in 1991.
  · Achieved continuous cost savings: initiated a change in film size.

Staff Artist   4/86-1/88
Acme Wiley Corporation, Signs and Systems, Elk Grove, IL
Designed architectural signage to meet specific client needs; utilized
building and zoning codes, as well as color and budgetary guidelines.
Produced signage brochures for custom signage programs.
Developed a company promotional brochure of signage options.
Created architectural and mechanical drawings, marker rendering
presentations and scale models for client programs.

Assistant Advertising Manager   4/85-1/86
Blue M, A unit of General Signal, Blue Island, IL
Planned, developed and distributed product brochures, catalogs and
informational pieces throughout the organization.
Placed advertisements in major trade publications and updated/maintained
customer mailing lists.

EDUCATION: ***Bachelor of Fine Arts, Graphic Design***
Ball State University, Muncie, IN

Formal Macintosh training through Black Dot Graphics, Crystal Lake, IL

RANDIE SLEEPER

1105 Orchard Avenue
Schaumburg, IL 60193   847/555-3678

HOSPITALITY MANAGEMENT / OPERATIONS

EXPERIENCE:

▶ Skilled in new business development for bar and kitchen operations, including full responsibility for staffing, sales and business administration.

▶ Coordinate budgets, inventories, purchasing and quality control for food, beverages and supplies; manage creative advertising, promotions and marketing, as well as entertainment services.

▶ Effectively hire, train, supervise and motivate staff and management in all bar procedures, food service activities and personal customer relations.

EMPLOYMENT: Ramada O'Hare / Marriott, Rosemont, IL   10/86-Present
Department Manager / Supervisor
In charge of virtually all operations in the sports bar and grill of this 723-room hotel, including training, scheduling and supervising a team of 12 in food/cocktail serving and bartending.
Constantly expand the customer base through creative planning and execution of promotions, PR and advertising, including special events, booking of disk jockeys, karaoke setups and contests.
Create and promote food and drink specials on a regular basis.
Work closely with vendors and suppliers and handle cost-effective purchasing, forecasting, budget control, payroll processing, bank deposits and purchase requests.
Utilize DTS and Remaco computer systems, and the DSS satellite system; familiar with Windows and MS Word.
TIPS Certified for alcohol intervention procedures.
→ Organize and/or design buffets, menus and in-house decorations.
→ Develop job descriptions and assign duties to appropriate staff.
→ Advanced from Server and Bartender to this position.
→ **Training through Marriott:** Completed and taught Marriott's Gold Standard Training; completed numerous courses in management, hospitality, motivation and communications, discipline and documentation.

Jimmy's Bar & Grill, Elmwood Park, IL
Manager   1984-1991
Effectively hired, trained and supervised a team of eight in direct customer service, upselling and the serving of food and beverages.

Bartender / Kitchen Crew   1982-1984
Responsible for all bartender duties including mixing drinks, working with customers, problem solving and maintaining sanitation.

VERONICA L. CHANDLER

2242 East Bryn Mawr Avenue
Roselle, IL 60172   630/555-3791

OBJECTIVE: ***INTERNSHIP***
A spring/summer internship where skills in communications, creative arts and environmental studies will be of value.

PROFILE: ■ Skilled in photography, poetry, radio production and newspaper reporting; trained in psychological and sociological issues, processes and techniques.

EDUCATION: Beloit College, Beloit, WI   1996-Present
Bachelor of Arts Degree Candidate
Major: Sociology   Minor: Environmental Studies
Award: W.C. Hooker Scholarship   AP Credit: Psychology

Courses:
Calculus
Elementary Japanese I & II
Introduction to Sociology
20th Century American Literature
Geological Hazards & Environmental Geology

Extracurricular Activities:
· WBCR weekly radio show D.J.
· BelSAC Floor Representative
· Intra-mural Soccer Team Player
· Bible Study Group Member
· Ballroom Dance Club Member
· Fall Ball Steering Committee

Work-Study: Physical Plant Worker/Recycling
Volunteer Service: Rockford Animal Shelter

Lake Park High School, Roselle, IL   Graduated 1996
GPA: 4.14/5.0

AP Classes: Psychology, Biology and World Literature and Composition
Participated in numerous activities including photography, newspaper reporter, Earth Club, Creative Arts Club, Marching Band Color Guard, Youth & Government, Psychology Club and Class Council.
Public Service: Proposed the establishment of a Teen Museum in Roselle and organized a poetry reading at the La Dolce Vita Cafe.

PART-TIME: **Cashier,** Pik-Kwik Foods, Roselle, IL   9/95-8/96
Sales Associate/Cashier, Wild Pair, Bloomingdale, Il   1/95-7/95

CHERYL CROWLEY

2044 Easton Court
Hanover Park, IL 60103

630/555-4760

MANAGEMENT TRAINEE

PROFILE:
- ▶ Proven abilities in supervision and training of associates, team development, cash management and customer service.
- ▶ Experienced in research, organization and presentation of data; skilled in Word, Excel, Windows 3.x and Windows 95.

EDUCATION:

<u>University of Iowa</u>, Iowa City, IA
Bachelor of Arts, History: Minor equivalency in Mathematics, Political Science and Chemistry.
Researched, compiled and organized data for several large-scale reports.
Tutored other students in French, Math, Chemistry and History.
→ Awarded a scholarship for studies during freshman year.
→ Served as Building Coordinator and Member of Residence Hall Government; coordinated several dance, sporting and fund-raising events.

EXPERIENCE:

<u>NorthWest Mosquito Abatement District</u>, Elk Grove, IL Summer 1996-1997
Inspector
Worked in a team environment to identify mosquito populations.
Documented stages of larvae development.
Safely handled equipment and various chemicals.

<u>Warner / Electric / Atlantic</u>, Bensenville, IL   Summer 1993, 1995
Responsible for general warehousing duties including inventory control, receiving and re-stocking.
Operated materials handling equipment.

<u>Radio Shack</u>, Bloomingdale, IL   Summer 1994
Retail Sales
Worked with customers to identify needs; discussed product features and benefits.
Handled customer inquiries and accepted orders.
Processed and submitted credit card and cell phone applications.
→ Professionally handled cash transactions, prepared bank deposits and closed store for daily business.

<u>Santa's Village</u>, East Dundee, IL   Summer 1990-1992
Lead Game Operator
Trained new employees on game operations; set daily work/relief schedules.
Handle customer relations and cash transactions in a professional manner.

STEPHEN A. SAVER

2456 Randall Ridge Drive
Elgin, IL 60123

847/555-6072

OBJECTIVE: A position utilizing EMT skills, such as medical assistant, phlebotomist or EKG, respiratory or emergency room technician.

PROFILE:
- Comprehensive skills as Paramedic and EMT, including emergency care such as defibrillation, IV therapy (venipuncture & phlebotomy), CPR and First Aid.

- Operate all major life support equipment and interpret EKG strips; perform triage and work closely with doctors, nurses and medical staff at all levels of experience.

- **Certified Paramedic and Firefighter II;** additional training in Biology, Chemistry, Anatomy and Physiology.

EMPLOYMENT: Hanover Park Fire Protection District, Hanover Park, IL   9/97-Present
Paramedic / Firefighter
Perform all aspects of emergency care in high-pressure, fast-paced situations, including patient defibrillation, bandaging and stabilization. Administer CPR as required and provide all essential life support services, prior to and during patient transport to various hospitals.

Pro-Care Ambulance Service, **EMT-B (Emergency Medical Technician)**
Superior Ambulance Service, and
American Medical Response/AMR, **EMT-B**
Located in Elgin, Elmhurst and Glendale Heights, IL   5/96-2/98

Ameritech, Inc., Elgin, IL   8/94-7/95
Telephone Technician
Communicated with customers on a daily basis and repaired/installed service through switches and the Ameritech infrastructure.

EDUCATION: John A. Logan Community College, Carterville, IL   1996
Major: EMT-B

Southern Illinois University, Carbondale, IL   1995-1996
Major: Biology

St. Francis Hospital, Evanston, IL
Paramedic Program   **Completed 1998**

MILITARY: U.S. Navy, San Diego, CA   1989-1992
Rate-Sonar Technician
Trained personnel in office procedures and operated various electronics.

ANITA PASTUKH

2290 Darby Lane
Roselle, IL 60172

630/555-5138

OBJECTIVE: *OFFICE ADMINISTRATION / MANUFACTURING OPERATIONS*
Accounting Functions or Production Scheduling

PROFILE:
- Experience in office administration and production scheduling activities, with attention to daily work order changes, work loads and job assignments.
- Hire, train and supervise employees in job procedures and adherence to quality; familiar with MS Word and Lotus 1-2-3 for Windows 95; bilingual in Polish/English and proficient in Russian.

EMPLOYMENT: Sweet Pea's Cleaning, Inc., Lombard, IL   1991-Present
Supervisor
Organize, coordinate and supervise multiple cleaning crews for this residential cleaning service, including job and route assignments, with responsibility for customer relations.
Hire, train and review the performance of new employees; maintain payroll records. Schedule daily appointments, with attention to special client instructions and work order changes.
Identify procedures to streamline operations and contain costs.
- Changed service delivery from an all-route, single van-operation to an owner-operator operation, whereby each employee drives to assigned clients directly.
- Accepted this position soon after relocating to the United States in 1990.

Juvenile Detention Home/Center, Bielsko-Biala, Poland   1989-1990
Teacher / Counselor
Instructed problematic and learning disabled children of ages 7 to 18, placed in this juvenile detention home by the Court.
- Counseled minors on substance abuse problems.
- Organized a summer camp, with daily recreational activities.
- Worked with LBD children on academic lessons and individualized therapeutic treatment plan goals for improvement.

Urzad Skarbowy, Bielsko-Biala, Poland   1984-1985
Accountant
Responsible for the processing and collection of tax payments from business owners.
Researched financial histories, to review for payments due.
Reconciled individual taxpayer monthly balances and prepared closing statements.
- Set up and maintained accounting records.

EDUCATION: College of DuPage, Glen Ellyn, IL
Attend English and English as a Second Language courses.   1997-Present
Slaski University, Katowice, Poland   1985-1989
Completed four years of a five-year undergraduate degree program in Social Work/Counseling, with a focus on youth development.
Liceum Ogolnoksztalcace, Kety, Poland   Graduated 1984
A college preparatory school.

GRACE STYLE

2217 Devon
Roselle, IL 60172   630/555-2263

PATIENT REGISTRATION / OFFICE ADMINISTRATION

PROFILE:
- ▶ Comprehensive experience in a wide range of administrative functions including patient registration, switchboard operations and data entry.

- ▶ Superior communication skills used to coordinate between various departments and provide patients with excellent service. Fluent in English and Italian; familiar with Spanish.

EXPERIENCE: Alexian Brothers Hospital, Elk Grove Village, IL   1995-Present
Patient Registration / Float Person
Responsible for all aspects of patient registration, including the entry of insurance information into a mainframe computer system.
Work in ER, Out-Patient and In-Patient registration areas.
Order blood and urine tests and register patients for various tests and procedures.
Coordinate with floor staff for bed assignments.
Take calls from physicians to reserve bed space and procedures for patients.

Switchboard / Admitting   1995-1996
Handled and routed all incoming calls to the hospital.
Wrote messages and paged doctors; relayed information from patients.
Updated codes in the computer system as required.

Parkway Bank and Trust, Elk Grove Village, IL   1993-1995
Universal Teller
Promoted to this position after three months. Responsible for the main vault with over $200,000. Handled all aspects of teller services including customer relations and cash management.

Home Federal Savings, Roselle, IL   1989-1991
Bank Teller
Provided customer service and handled cash and financial transactions.

Jorgensen Steel Company, Schaumburg, IL   1987-1988
File Clerk (Temporary)
Responsible for various office functions including data entry and file management.

Nitram Metal, Elk Grove Village, IL   1987
General Office (Part-time)
Performed a wide range of office work such as file maintenance, data entry and reception.

EDUCATION: Graduated from Lake View High School   1987

MATHEW PIC

2215 Lincoln
Glendale Heights, IL 60139   708/555-7187

PIC SUPERVISOR

EXPERIENCE:
- More than nine years in production operations including responsibility for line setup, management and quality control.
- Skilled in strategic planning, MRP, budgets and forecasting; coordinate purchasing, JIT, cost-effective inventory control and cycle counts.
- Strong background in A.P.I.C.S. requirements and safety/housekeeping inspections.
- Hire, train, supervise and motivate production teams and foremen in procedures and operations; fluent in Spanish and English.

EMPLOYMENT: Suncast Corporation, Batavia, IL   1981-Present
PIC Supervisor
Responsible for all aspects of production and inventory control in the manufacture of various lawn and garden supplies.
Effectively hire, train and supervise five foremen on three shifts; indirectly responsible for 15 line workers; currently on 24-hour call.
Plan and schedule jobs for molding and assembly in a cost-effective manner.
Involved in molding and assembly operations with more than 35 mold presses.
Coordinate MRP and update/maintain accurate inventories on PRAXA software on a VAX/VMS system; supervise WIP inventories on a regular basis.
* Developed a strong team atmosphere among virtually all personnel.
* Maintain excellent product quality through communication with the customer service department.
* Coordinate/purchase projects through outside manufacturers and vendors.
* Work directly with engineers; organize shipping and receiving for parts and product lines.

Materials Control Foreman	1990-1991
Leadman Chosen as Employee of the Month.	1988-1989
Furniture Production Foreman	1984-1987
Assistant Foreman, Furniture Department	1982-1984
Machine Operator	1981-1982

EDUCATION: Waubonsee Community College, Sugar Grove, IL   11/92-Present
Attending courses in APICS Standards.

Aurora College, Aurora, IL   Supervisory Management Certificate 1991

College of DuPage, Glen Ellyn, IL   1984-1988
Completed various courses including Business.

CAINE LAIT

225 Berry Lane
Streamwood, IL 60107   630/555-2330

PRODUCTION OPERATIONS / MATERIAL ANALYST

PROFILE:
▶ Comprehensive experience in manufacturing and procedure documentation, as well as staff training in product assembly and troubleshooting.

▶ Communicate with customers and suppliers on product updates; work closely with staff, management and suppliers for status reporting and in-process changes.

▶ Experience with MS Excel, Word and PowerPoint for inventory control, data entry, spreadsheet updating and correspondence.

EXPERIENCE: Motorola, Inc., Schaumburg, IL   11/88-Present
Material Analyst and Instructor / Trainer
Responsible for in-plant transfers of production materials, including posting, receiving and resolving a wide range of issues related to circuit board production.
Perform group and individual training of new hires, including documentation of progress, liaison between supervisors and the training department.

→ Directly involved in writing and updating Manufacturing Process Standards (MPS) for postwave, mechanical assembly, board test and repair, with detailed, step-by-step procedures for each area.

→ As **Team Leader,** tracked daily production versus production goals, requiring constant involvement with customers and suppliers.

→ Involved in initiating the cellular educational training program, with an emphasis on problem solving.

Motorola Training includes:
APD Safety Fundamentals, The Ownership Spirit, Windows 3.1, Diversity Awareness, Wingz 1.1, Framemaker 4.0, MPC, Factory Control System (APD), Surface Mount Technology, Individual Dignity Entitlement for Employees; Lotus 1-2-3, Introduction to DOS, POPI, Effective Team Leadership, Problem Solving, Right to Know, CMO Performance Review Training, New Job Skill Training, Beginning Symphony and Interaction for Manufacturing Employees.

CERTIFICATIONS
and DUTIES: Soldering, Testing, Assembly and Repair, Team Trainer, Material Handling, including posting, receiving, pick requests and troubleshooting for Location 77.

Sealed Power Corporation, Des Plaines, IL   1981-1988
Zenith Corporation, Chicago, IL   1976-1978

EDUCATION: Malcolm X City College, Major: Accounting

Elgin Community College, Attending courses in English, Writing and Typing.

RACHELLE MEMO

2348 Hesterman Drive
Glendale Heights, IL 60139
708/555-7778

OBJECTIVE: *RECEPTIONIST:* A position where proven communication skills and attention to detail would be utilized.

PROFILE:
- More than three years in various business environments, including customer service, office support and the reconciliation of reports for purchasing and inventory control.
- Handle telephone communications in a professional manner, as well as message taking and data entry/retrieval; balance cash transactions with speed and accuracy.
- Proficient in Windows, Paradox and WordPerfect 5.1.

EMPLOYMENT: Tri Star Metals, Inc., Carol Stream, IL   4/94-Present
Office Clerk
Provide a wide range of office services in a professional manner, including data entry/retrieval of purchase orders utilizing Paradox.
Analyze and update monthly purchase order and inventory reports.
- Perform proofreading, verification and distribution of invoices.
- Conduct research to resolve discrepancies.
- Compile documentation for freight bills.

Footlocker, Bloomingdale, IL   5/92-4/94
Cashier
Responsible for customer service and sales transactions for this high-volume shoe retail outlet.
Accurately handled large amounts of cash.
- Operated a computerized register system.
- Trained a new employee in professional customer service, store procedures, product lines and register operations.
- Processed returns and exchanges on a daily basis.

Phar-Mor, Inc., Bloomingdale, IL   8/91-5/92
Duties similar to those at Footlocker including training, customer service and computerized register transactions.
- Balanced daily register receipts.

EDUCATION: College of DuPage, Glen Ellyn, IL   Attending part-time
Associates Degree in Arts expected May, 2000

Glenbard North High School, Carol Stream, IL   1992

KAREN R. HEADSET
671 Rodenburg Road #304
Roselle, IL 60172
708/555-3201

RECEPTIONIST / OFFICE SUPPORT

EXPERIENCE:
- Skilled in general reception, switchboard operation and customer service, as well as personal communications in fast-paced environments.

- Familiar with Windows, Windows WordPerfect and Excel for customer correspondence, spreadsheets and status reports.

EMPLOYMENT:

Sunbeam Household Products, Schaumburg, IL   11/95-2/96
Receptionist
Responsible for switchboard operation and telephone answering for 90 extensions.
Communicate with customers, answer questions, and expedite messages.
Compile and print purchase orders and requisitions; handle incoming and outgoing faxes, copying and filing.
* Coordinate travel plans and schedules for staff and managers.

Centennial Executive Suites, Schaumburg, IL   1993-1995
Switchboard Operator
Answered hundreds of calls daily for up to 43 companies in shared executive suites.
Greeted visitors, notified clients of appointments and delivered mail.

ERA Abbott Real Estate, Schaumburg, IL   1992-1993
Secretary
Duties included reception and switchboard operation for up to 60 agents.

Remcor Products Company, Glendale Heights, IL   1990-1991
Receptionist
Operated a switchboard for up to 200 employees.
Performed data entry/retrieval of credit memos and processed accounts receivable for the company register.

Builders Plumbing Supply, Addison, IL   1989-1990
Receptionist
Handled four telephone lines for 300 employees, greeted customers, and sorted, prepared and distributed daily mail; operated the postage machine accurately.

Suburban Computer Services, Palatine, IL   1987-1989
Receptionist

EDUCATION:

College of DuPage, Glen Ellyn, IL   Graduated 1987
A.A. Degree: Office Management

Schaumburg High School, Schaumburg, IL   Graduated 1985

OLIVIA K. WRECKTEAM

2247 Georgetown Drive
Carol Stream, IL 50188   Res: 630/555-4343

RECREATION SUPERVISOR

PROFILE:
- ▸ Plan and implement programs, projects and special activities for large organizations; serve as liaison with companies and their employees.

- ▸ Experience in youth development, childcare and parenting functions, with full responsibility for daily recreational, educational and social activities in family, childcare center and social agency environments.

- ▸ Skilled in motor skill and social interaction development, especially with behavioral learning and developmentally disabled children; handle multiple priorities and communicate sensitive issues to children, parents and staff tactfully.

- ▸ B.S. degree in park and recreation studies, with a minor in law enforcement; formerly certified in CPR and First Aid; volunteer youth counselor/teacher.

EMPLOYMENT:
Chicago Title & Trust, Carol Stream, IL   11/97-Present
Searcher, Special Search Department
Conduct computerized tract searches, including extensive communication with attorneys, property owners and utility companies seeking information recorded on or against subject properties.
→ Launched the company's first coed softball team.
→ Instituted a blood drive through Heartland.

Central DuPage Hospital, Winfield, IL   2/92-11/97
Shift Supervisor, Surgical Department
Hired, trained and evaluated department personnel and acted as employee liaison to management; organized, directed and reviewed work.

Sterilization Tech II, Surgical Department
→ Hospital representative for the United Way campaign.

**COMMUNITY
SERVICE:**
Faith Covenant Church, Wheaton, IL
- Counselor, Church High League Winter Retreat
- Youth Counselor, ages 8-9, Pioneer Club
- Sunday School Teacher, Preschool, ages 4-5

EDUCATION:
College of DuPage, Glen Ellyn, IL   current
Certification program: Elementary Education

Western Illinois University, Macomb, IL   1986
B.S. Degree in Parks and Recreation; Minor: Law Enforcement
Twelve-week Internship: Cunningham Children's Home, Urbana, IL
Volunteer, Macomb Rehabilitation Center: improved children's motor skills.

MICHAEL SCANNER

11227 N. Overhill
Chicago, IL 60631

773/555-1576

SCANNER / MAC OPERATOR

EXPERIENCE:
- More than nine years in lithography including full responsibility for Macintosh assembly and plotting.
- Specialize in advanced film output and color separations; handle color correction, enlargements, reductions & stretches.
- Utilize Macintosh, Scitex and Rampage systems, the 340 Hell Scanner and 2-color silkscreen presses. Working knowledge of QuarkXpress and Illustrator; familiar with PhotoShop, FreeHand and PageMaker.

EMPLOYMENT: Compo Graphics, Chicago, IL   4/98-1/99
Mac Operator
Responsible for preflight, assembly and output of four to six color files.
Perform plotting on the Dolev 4-press.
Responsible for the quality of films and proofs.

Electronic Prepress Services, Arlington Heights, IL   10/93-4/98
Mac Operator
Responsible for preflight, assembly and output of four to six color files.
Handled plotting on Dolev 400 and 800 output devices.
* Promoted to this position from Plotter Operator.

The Color Company, Elk Grove Village, IL   8/89-6/93
Apprentice Scanner Operator
Responsible for prompt, accurate scanning of transparencies and reflective art for Condé Nast publications including House & Garden, Glamour, Vogue and Mademoiselle magazines.
Trained one employee in proofing, vertical camera work, the 340 Hell and the Crossfield system.
* Matched and/or improved subjects; handled all aspects of enlargements, reductions and stretches.

TCR Graphics, Streamwood, IL   11/88-8/89
Proofer / Camera Operator

EDUCATION: Triton College, River Grove, IL   1990
Successful completion of a course in Offset Printing.
* Awarded Apprenticeship for Journeyman Status.

Harper College, Palatine, IL.
Completed a course in QuarkXpress

Hoffman Estates High School, Hoffman Estates, IL   Graduated 1986

YVETTE M. SPEAKER

2200 Lacy Avenue
Streamwood, IL 60107   630/555-3949

OBJECTIVE: ***TEACHER'S AIDE***
Elementary and Middle School Levels

PROFILE:

▶ Skilled in problem identification and resolution with attention to detail; proven ability to focus on the learning needs of children and obtain appropriate assistance, materials and resources.

▶ Work well with groups and individuals from diverse backgrounds; actively participate in school and neighborhood meetings, programs and events; strong work ethic and desire to nurture students to achieve their potential.

**RELATED
EXPERIENCE:**   Heritage Elementary School, Streamwood, IL   10/96-present
Volunteer Parent
- *Book Fair:* Set up and disassemble the exhibit area, display books and advise children on their book selections.
- *Lunch Supervisor:* serve parents and students lunches and monitor activities.

Involved in numerous parent-child and neighborhood activities:
- Christmas drama productions
- Walk-a-thon for Kid's Play
- Roger's Park Neighborhood Police Department public service meetings on gangs, drugs and youth development issues.

EMPLOYMENT: Standard Parking, Inc., Chicago, IL   1988-9/96
Cashier, Prudential Plaza Garage
Handled individual cash and automatic card parking ticket transactions daily. Answered telephone calls and responded to inquiries about rates and hours. Resolved fee and service discrepancies accurately, promptly and tactfully. Worked closely with security and the senior manager to resolve customer problems and emergencies dealing with such matters as lost keys, broken door locks, tire changes and dead batteries.
Reconciled cash receipts and prepared a Cashier Report for the senior manager.

U.S. Post Office, Chicago, IL   Seasonal, 1987-1988
Casual Employee

EDUCATION: Harry S Truman College, Chicago, IL   1986-1988
Completed A.A. Degree-level coursework in child development.

John F. Kennedy High School, Chicago, IL   Graduated 1986

Job Hunt Resource Materials

Listings, catalogs and great books

Many of the books and resources listed in this Appendix can make researching companies quick and easy. They cross-reference companies by industry and provide insight on company size and products, as well as names of human resource personnel and key managers. Many of these are listed in John Lucht's book *Rites of Passage at $100,000+*. Ask your business librarian about listings and reference materials specific to your industry: light or heavy manufacturing, construction, tool & die, mold makers, etc.

Commerce Register's Geographical Directories of Manufacturer's. Numerous directories for specific geographical regions. Organized by city, this book provides information on manufacturers with more than five employees in the state or region, including address, telephone, products, and sales figures.

Corporate 1000 Yellow Book, International Corporate 1000 Yellow Book and *Over-The-Counter 1000 Yellow Book.* By Monitor Publishing Co. Each lists names, titles, and, often, direct-dial numbers for key officers, plus outside board members and their companies.

Directories in Print. By Gale Research, Inc. Published every two years. Companies are organized by industry/discipline. Describes the contents of 10,000 publications including directories, professional and scientific rosters, and other lists and guides.

Electronic Resumes. Wayne Gonyea and James Gonyea. McGraw Hill, New York, 1995. This book covers all the essentials on developing and posting an electronic resume. Wayne helped set up my company's Web site, and is one of the leaders in online career resources. His company is Online Solutions, Inc. and his site is at: ResumeXpress.com.

Electronic Resumes & Online Networking. Rebecca Smith, Career Press. An accessible guide to using the Internet as an effective resume networking tool.

Encyclopedia of Business Information Sources. Gale Research, Inc. More than 20,000 information sources on 1,280 highly specific subjects ranging from *abrasives* to *zinc*. Lists encyclopedias, dictionaries, handbooks, manuals, bibliographies, associations, societies, etc.

Guide to American Directories. By B. Klein Publications. Updated every two years. Describes content, frequency, and cost (if any) of 7,500 directories in a variety of fields (more than 300 classifications) with phone numbers.

Job Hunter's Resource Guide. Gale Research, Inc. Annual, one volume. Lists reference materials for 150 specific professions and occupations. Also has a "how-to" section.

Job Seeker's Guide to Public and Private Companies. Gale Research, Inc. Information on more than 25,000 companies, including corporate overviews, specific job titles and estimated number of openings for each, hiring practices, personnel contacts, employee benefits, application procedures, and recruitment activities.

Million Dollar Directory Series. Dun's Marketing Services. A five-volume hard-cover series listing 160,000 public and private U.S. companies. Includes key facts on decision-makers, company size, and lines of business. This may be hard to find, considering its $1,250 annual lease fee.

The National Directory of Addresses and Telephone Numbers. General Information, Inc. Great for your mailing list. Provides addresses and phone numbers for U.S. corporations, both alphabetically and by S.I.C. category.

101 Great Answers to the Toughest Interview Questions. Ron Fry, Career Press. A useful guide to the interview process identifying the most commonly asked interview questions, and offering great answers.

The Smart Woman's Guide to Interviewing and Salary Negotiations. Julie Adair King, Careeer Press. Sound strategies that anyone can use when preparing for job interviews, and striving to get the best salary possible.

The Smart Woman's Guide to Resumes and Job Hunting. Betsy Sheldon and Julie Adair King, Career Press. <u>Not</u> for women only. It's packed with practical advice on developing a resume—especially when you have challenges such as gaps in work histroy or have been out of the work force for awhile.

Success 2000. By Vicki Spina and Dearborn Publishing. Published in January, 1993 and available by mail order outside the Chicago area: 1-800-247-6553.

Thomas' Register of American Manufacturers. Thomas Publishing Company. Annual profile of 150,000 manufacturers with their major products and services. Includes 12,000 pages of catalog material and 112,000 registered trade/brand names.

Unlimited Power. Anthony Robbins. A great book by the guru of communication and getting yourself together.

Ward's Business Directory of U.S. Private and Public Companies. Gale Research, Inc. Annual, four volumes. Provides demographic and financial business data on over 85,000 companies. Volumes provide alphabetic and zip-code listings of companies.

Index

About the Author

Steven A. Provenzano, CPRW, is president of A Advanced Resume Service, Inc. He is author of five career books, including *Blue Collar Resumes*.

Free resume price quote

With expanding use of the Internet, my career books, fax and e-mail, we've written resumes for clients all over the U.S., and in just about every country in the world. I'll be happy to review your resume, give basic feedback, and quote an exact price for writing your custom resume. We conduct a personal interview with you over the phone (the call's on us within the U.S.) and write a high-impact resume for you in one to three working days. After you proofread and finalize the content, we can mail you 10 laser prints on quality paper, and/or send it out on disk, or e-mail directly to your home.

For your free resume price quote and feedback, simply fax, mail, or e-mail your resume to us, then call at the numbers listed below and we'll discuss your options. Here's how to reach us:

Steven A. Provenzano / CPRW
A ADVANCED Resume Service, Inc.
701 E. Irving Park Road #201
Roselle, IL 60172

Phone: 630/582-1088   24-hour fax: 630/582-1105
E-mail: ADVRESUMES@aol.com
Or visit our Web site at:
crm21.com/advanced/advanced.html

We accept Visa, MasterCard, American Express, and Discover.